Justin Bonello's
ULTIMATE
BRAAI
MASTER

BASED ON SEASON ONE OF THE TV SERIES

Penguin Books

PENGUIN BOOKS

Published by the Penguin Group

Penguin Books (South Africa) (Pty) Ltd, Block D,
Rosebank Office Park, 181 Jan Smuts Avenue, Parktown North
Johannesburg 2193, South Africa

Penguin Group (USA) Inc, 375 Hudson Street, New York,
New York 10014, USA

Penguin Group (Canada), 90 Eglinton Avenue East, Suite 700,
Toronto, Ontario, Canada M4P 2Y3 (a division of Pearson
Penguin Canada Inc)

Penguin Books Ltd, 80 Strand, London WC2R 0RL, England

Penguin Ireland, 25 St Stephen's Green, Dublin 2, Ireland
(a division of Penguin Books Ltd)

Penguin Group (Australia), 2707 Collins Street, Melbourne,
Victoria 3008, Australia (a division of Pearson Australia
Group Pty Ltd)

Penguin Books India Pvt Ltd, 11 Community Centre,
Panchsheel Park, New Delhi – 110 017, India

Penguin Group (NZ), 67 Apollo Drive, Rosedale, Auckland
0632, New Zealand (a division of Pearson New Zealand Ltd)

Penguin Books (South Africa) (Pty) Ltd, Registered Offices:
Block D, Rosebank Office Park, 181 Jan Smuts Avenue,
Parktown North Johannesburg 2193, South Africa

www.penguinbooks.co.za

First published by Penguin Books (South Africa) (Pty) Ltd 2012

Copyright © Justin Bonello 2012

All rights reserved

The moral right of the author has been asserted

ISBN 978-0-14-353045-9

Written by Justin Bonello and Helena Lombard

Contributors: Bertus Basson, Marthinus Ferreira
and the Ultimate Braai Master Teams

Recipe testing by Janet Gird

Photography by Louis Hiemstra

Food styling by Caroline Gardner

Cover photograph by Duane Howard

Design and layout by twoshoes.co.za

Printed and bound by CTP Printers, Cape Town

Contents

Introduction

In every group of friends across the length and breadth of South Africa, there is always one Braai Master, that girl or guy that we trust to hold the tongs and create memories around a fire. Problem is, in that circle of friends, we rarely get any new blood with new ideas so, year in and year out, rain or shine, we braai the same lamb chops, the same chook and use the same tricks of the trade.

Our braai universe has remained unchanged . . . until now.

The Ultimate Braai Master throws together a bunch of braai masters from all walks of life, drawn from the rainbow nation, each with different skills sets, backgrounds and mindsets. Suddenly the braai universe opens up!

We all have that favourite way of dishing up great food from the fire, but I have the teams that took part in this inaugural TV series to thank for shattering my braai world. I always thought that I was at the top of my game, but this group of people made me realise that I am not a Braai Master – not yet, anyway – and that I'm still learning. I hope this book helps you to learn a little as well.

A word of warning: this book is not just about the road trippers, about the food they made, nor is it about the challenges they faced. This book is also about the braai road trip of a lifetime and how this group of now new friends got to see and experience the incredible places in South Africa that many of us only get to dream about.

I hope you enjoy the ride . . . and, who knows, maybe you will become the next Ultimate Braai Master.

START YOUR FIRES

U B

M

THE ULTIMATE BRAAI MASTER

Dayle

FAT COW
FRIENDS

Warwick

GAL POWER
SISTERS

Lethu

Sindi

JanieB

Maudie

WHICH WAY BRAAI CHICKS
FRIENDS

MARTHINUS FERREIRA
CHEF
BRAAI MASTER JUDGE

JUSTIN BONELLO
COOK
BRAAI MASTER HOST

BERTUS BASSON
CHEF
BRAAI MASTER JUDGE

Lee

Barry

Roxanne

POPEYE & OLIVE
FATHER & DAUGHTER

COAL SHOULDER
ENGAGED

Roger

Leki

Tinus

THE GREEN FEET TEAM
FRIENDS

Sebastian

2M
FRIENDS

Dumisani

ORANGE RIVER
U B
M
NAMIBIAN BORDER

OUR ULTIMATE BRAAI ROAD TRIP KICKS OFF IN NAMIBIA IN THE SOUTH WEST OF AFRICA. EVERY TIME I COME HERE, I'M AMAZED AT HOW, ONCE YOU'VE DEALT WITH THE (MOSTLY DISGRUNTLED AND SERIOUSLY UNHAPPY-LOOKING) CUSTOMS OFFICIALS AND CROSSED THE BORDER, THE ENERGY AND LANDSCAPE CHANGE THE MOMENT YOU DRIVE ON TO THE BRIDGE AND OVER THE ORANGE RIVER. IN A COUNTRY WHERE THERE ARE ONLY 2.1 PEOPLE PER SQUARE KILOMETRE YOU CAN JUST IMAGINE HOW VAST THE LANDSCAPES ARE. EVEN THOUGH SOUTH AFRICA MIGHT STILL BE TEASING YOU IN YOUR CAR'S REAR-VIEW MIRROR, YOU'LL SOON FORGET ABOUT IT WHEN YOU SEE WHAT'S IN FRONT OF YOU. THE MOUNTAINS LOOK JAGGED AND UNFORGIVING – ALMOST AS IF THEY'VE EXPLODED OUT OF THE EARTH – AND YOU MIGHT THINK THAT SOMEHOW YOU'VE JUST LANDED ON THE MOON. IN FACT, IT'S THE IDEAL PLACE TO CHEAT A 'MOON LANDING', AND TO ME, THE DEEPER YOU DRIVE INTO THE ARID LANDSCAPE, THE MORE IT BECOMES THE PERFECT SETTING FOR AN EERIE APOCALYPTIC SCENE.

IN SUCH A VAST COUNTRY, IT'S EASY TO THINK THAT YOU'RE COMPLETELY ISOLATED AND I WAS TEMPTED TO KEEP DRIVING FURTHER INLAND, BUT WE WERE HEADED ON A DIFFERENT ADVENTURE AT THE FELIX UNITE RIVER CAMP IN AN AREA CALLED NOORDOEWER, SET ON THE BANKS OF THE ORANGE RIVER (OR NU GARIEP, AS IT WAS KNOWN TO THE BUSHMEN).

THE ORANGE RIVER IS OUR COUNTRY'S MOST IMPRESSIVE AND FROM ITS
SOURCE IN THE MOUNTAIN KINGDOM OF LESOTHO IT FLOWS FOR ROUGHLY
2000 KILOMETRES THROUGH THE MOST ARID PARTS OF SOUTHERN AFRICA
AND IS A BEACON OF HOPE AND LIFE TO MANY. THE RIVER ENDS ITS JOURNEY
IN THE ATLANTIC OCEAN AT THE DIAMOND MINING TOWNS OF ALEXANDER BAY
AND ORANJEMUND. BUT OUR ADVENTURE DOESN'T COVER 2000 KILOMETRES
BY WATER. FELIX UNITE RIVER CAMP IS ONLY THE STARTING POINT – A PLACE
OF WHICH I HAVE FOND MEMORIES OF DAYS PADDLING DOWNSTREAM WITH
FRIENDS AND NIGHTS CAMPING ON THE BANKS OF THE RIVER WHERE THE ONLY
SOUNDS YOU'LL HEAR ARE THOSE OF THE FIRE CRACKLING AND THE BOTTLE OF
OLD BROWN BEING PASSED AROUND. THE REST IS SILENCE AND STARS.

RULE NUMBER ONE OF BRAAIING: DON'T INTERFERE WITH THE TONG MASTER. WHEN YOU DO THAT, IT GIVES HIM PERMISSION TO TURN HIS BACK ON YOU AND BOOT YOU OUT OF THE BRAAI CIRCLE . . . AND NO ONE WANTS TO BE BOOTED OUT BECAUSE YOU'LL END UP MAKING SALAD IN THE KITCHEN. NUMBER TWO? DON'T EVEN THINK ABOUT STANDING AROUND THE FIRE WITHOUT A DRINK IN YOUR HAND. IT'S DEFINITELY ILLEGAL AND IS MOREOVER AN INTEGRAL PART OF ANY BRAAI AND IF YOU'RE LUCKY ALL YOUR (MORE IRRESPONSIBLE) FRIENDS WILL STILL BE STANDING BY THE TIME THE FOOD IS READY. SHOULD YOU FIND THEM SWAGGERING AROUND AIMLESSLY, MUMBLING INCOHERENTLY AND LOOKING A BIT GLASSY EYED, FEED THEM TILL THEY EITHER SOBER UP OR THEIR EYES BECOME DROOPY AND THEY PASS OUT ON YOUR COUCH (AGAIN).

ORANGE RIVER

Yaka

This is my version of Yucca, a drink which contains vodka, lemons and lime. You can use whatever citrus is available, and if you're not a fan of the cane train, use vodka or gin instead.

First up, cut the peeled oranges and grapefruit into segments, plonk them in the plastic container, then take a potato masher (or any other handy 'bashing' tool) and moer the fruit into submission until you have something that resembles chunky juice. Now pour the entire bottle of cane into the chunky juice, add cup of sugar and the zest and stir it around until it is well mixed. Cover with a lid and set aside in a cool spot to infuse for a couple of hours (preferably somewhere out of reach of your friends).

When your friends arrive (and if they look thirsty and moody after a long week), strain the juice through a sieve into a jug. Top with ice and lemonade or soda water (depending on how sweet your tooth is) and make their day better.

You can also skip the straining and keep the juice chunky if you like – that's the way I like it.

ULTIMATE BRAAI RECIPE!
JUSTIN BONELLO

YOU'LL NEED:
the juice and zest of about 10
oranges and 8 grapefruit
1 cup of white sugar
1 bottle of cane
a big plastic container with a lid

THIS IS A REFRESHING BREW THAT YOU CAN EASILY PACK INTO A COOLER BAG AND TAKE WITH YOU ON A CAMPING ROAD TRIP. IT'S A REVIVING DRINK ON A HOT DAY IN THE GREAT OUTDOORS.

Pineapple BEER

YOU'LL NEED:
- 2 pineapples
- 6 litres of lukewarm water
- 2 cups of sugar (or less if the pineapple is very sweet)
- ½ cup of raisins
- a chunk of ginger – sliced (you want about 2 tablespoons)
- 10 g packet of dried yeast
- a large plastic container
- glass bottles with screw caps

Take a clean sponge-scourer and, using the rough side (the side you would use on a dirty pot), scrub the pineapples until all the thorny bits have been removed. Cut off the stalk (or crown), then slice the pineapple into small chunks (skin and all). Chuck the chunks of pineapple, water, sugar, raisins and ginger into a large plastic container or even a clean cooler box. Stir it around, sprinkle the dried yeast over the top and leave to stand for 30 minutes, then stir it again. Pop the lid on and let the beer ferment for 24 hours. Finally, strain into glass bottles and leave to stand for another 12 hours – and only then do you screw the caps on.

Store the pineapple beer in a dry, cool place and let it stand for 2 weeks. The best part of this recipe is watching your friends' faces when they unscrew the caps – some of the beer is bound to spray into their faces, clothes and hair – especially if you road tripped with it in the back of your car . . . like I did.

ULTIMATE BRAAI RECIPE · JUSTIN BONELLO

Smoky PUMPKIN SOUP

THIS IS GREAT AS A STARTER, BUT IF YOU WANT TO HAVE IT AS YOUR DINNER, ADD SAMP AND BEANS TO THE SOUP AND SERVE WITH FRESHLY BAKED BRUSCHETTA (PAGE 67).

 FOR 6 PEOPLE YOU'LL NEED:
- 1 pumpkin – kept whole
- 350 g butter
- 2 onions – chopped
- milk (how much you add depends on how thick you want the soup to be)
- salt and pepper

First up, make a fire, and when the coals are at a low heat, place the pumpkin straight on top of them. Leave it to braai for about 2 hours, turning it from time to time and adding more coals as necessary. Remove the pumpkin from the fire (I'll let you figure out how to do this without burning your hands) and when it has cooled down to touching temperature, cut it in half and scoop out the seeds to use later. Dig out as much of the flesh as possible. Cut it into cubes and put it in a bowl.

Next, place a flat-bottomed potjie on top of a braai grid or on a tripod, about 10 centimetres above the coals of a medium to hot fire. Melt the butter, add the onions and sauté until soft. Put the cubes of pumpkin into the potjie, pour over a couple of glugs of milk and season with salt and cracked black pepper to taste. Cover and let the soup simmer for about 20 minutes, stirring it every now and then to prevent it from burning.

TOPPINGS

While the soup is on the go, you can quickly whip up some toppings. Whatever you choose to put on top of your soup is just as important as what you put inside it, but plan it carefully, because it can either make or break the dish. Here are some ideas.

• PEANUTS
Take your trusty mortar and pestle, whack in some peanuts (salted or plain) and give them a good bashing.

• PARMESAN CROUTONS
Break a quarter of a loaf of bread into smallish chunks, drizzle with olive oil and mix. Add a handful of grated Parmesan and toss again. Whack some butter in a pan, add the bread chunks and fry them until golden brown and crispy.

• TOASTED PUMPKIN SEEDS
Take the seeds you put aside earlier, boil them in water for a few minutes, then strain through a sieve. Remove any stringy bits of pumpkin still stuck on the seeds, put them in a pan and add a pinch of salt and paprika or curry powder. Fry them for a couple of minutes until crispy.

• CRÈME FRAICHE
Add a small drizzle of truffle oil to crème fraiche and then whisk in some lemon zest.

By now the 20 minutes of simmering should be up and you can finish off the soup. Remove the potjie from the heat and squash the pumpkin, milk and onions as finely as you can with a potato masher. If the soup is too thick, add another splash of milk and stir, then push the mixture through a sieve, reheat the soup and then you're ready to serve.

Ladle into soup bowls, top with a spoonful of crème fraiche, Parmesan croutons and a sprinkle of peanuts and pumpkin seeds. *Lekker.*

THIS IS A GREAT SALAD, ESPECIALLY FOR THOSE LAZY AND LESS HUNGRY WARM DAYS OR NIGHTS, BECAUSE IT'S A MEAL IN ONE THAT WON'T LEAVE YOU FEELING STUFFED AND GASPING FOR AIR AFTERWARDS.

RUBBED SIRLOIN
and Crushed Potato
SALAD

First up, combine all the rub spices in your trusty mortar and pestle and give them a good bashing. Rub the ground spices into the meat until generously coated and leave to rest in the fridge for a couple of hours. Once your braai is ready and your guests are getting hungry, whack the sirloin on to your braai-grid (hot coals) and grill on an open flame for about 7 minutes a side. You want the meat to be medium rare. While the steaks are sizzling, it's time to start combining the salad – but remember to keep one eye on the meat!

Crush the cooked potatoes using the palm of your hand. You just want the skin to break open and to crush the potatoes lightly – try not to flatten them completely – this is not a pancake-potato salad. Add the chopped onions, capers, anchovies, olives and parsley. Drizzle with olive oil, a generous squeeze of lemon and cracked black pepper. Taste it before adding salt because the anchovies are very salty.

Mix the salad thoroughly then scoop on to plates. When the meat is done, let it rest for a few minutes then cut it into slices about 1 cm thick. Put a couple of slices of that deliciously juicy sirloin on top of the potato salad and you're done.

FOR THE RUB:
- 50 g whole coriander
- 25 g peppercorns
- 50 g mustard seeds
- 30 g coarse salt
- 15 g paprika

FOR THE SALAD:
- 2 pieces of matured sirloin steak, weighing about 200 g each
- 800 g baby potatoes – cooked in their skins
- 50 g onions – chopped
- 30 g capers – chopped
- 50 g anchovies – chopped
- 90 g olives – pips removed and quartered
- 30 g parsley – chopped
- olive oil
- freshly squeezed lemon juice
- black pepper and coarse sea salt

Fireside Pastry

RONEL CALLS THIS 'MAGIC PASTRY', BECAUSE THE SECRET TO MAKING THIS PUDDING IS TO HAVE COLD HANDS AND COLD INGREDIENTS THE WHOLE TIME, OTHERWISE THE PASTRY WON'T PUFF. LUCKY FOR RONEL HER HANDS WERE FREEZING AFTER HOURS OF PADDLING DOWN THE ORANGE RIVER (IN MID-WINTER) JUST BEFORE SHE MADE THIS DESSERT.

Wipe your camping table clean with a damp cloth and while it's drying go wash your hands in the river (if you're lucky enough to be near one). *Gooi* the flour straight on to the surface of the table, but make sure it's not in a windy spot or you'll end up with flour in your face and ears. Next, grab a cheese grater out of your camping toolbox (the one your wife insisted on packing) and grate the butter over the flour followed by the cream cheese, then work it into a dough using your very cold hands. Don't take any short cuts – when you grate the butter and cheese you give the pastry the air it needs.

FOR THE PASTRY, YOU'LL NEED:

- 250 ml white flour
- 250 ml butter
- 250 ml cream cheese (any type that's firm enough to grate)

Now comes the only tricky part: for the pastry to work you're going to need to chill it for a couple of hours or preferably overnight. When Ronel made this, she didn't have access to a fridge and had to make do with ice and a cooler box out of the sun. She didn't have the luxury of time either, and kept it cold while working with it by putting the dough into a bowl and straight on to ice until she had to use it.

Take small balls of dough one at a time (kick the cooler box closed in between balls of dough – it needs to stay cold). Sprinkle some flour on to that same camping table then roll the dough out using an empty wine bottle from the night before. The dough shouldn't be too thick (roughly 1 mm). Once you have six or more oddly shaped pastries in front of you, you're almost ready. Shape pieces of foil into cups – as big or as small as you want. Place the pastry inside the foil, pressing down so it takes the shape of the cup then pop it back into the cooler box.

★ COKE, HONEY AND LEMON REDUCTION

Ronel made this reduction, but I like my pastries without it.

Take a fire-friendly pot, put it over medium-hot coals and pour in a couple of glugs of Coca-Cola. Add a squirt of honey (it helps the Coke reduce) and a good squeeze of lemon. Let it simmer until it becomes syrupy. Once done and cooled down, take the pastry out of the cooler box (again) and scoop about a teaspoon of the reduction on top of the pastry. Yes, you now pop it back on to the ice again.

★ THE FILLING

You can fill the pastries with whatever you like. Ronel likes to add banana as one of her favourites. Me? I'm partial to sliced apples fried in cinnamon, butter and sugar. So, peel and chop up your favourite fruit into chunks (any size you like). Take the pastry out of the cooler box (this is the last time, I promise) and pack your choice of fruit inside (either pre-cooked, like mine, or raw like Ronel's). Mix together brown sugar and cinnamon and sprinkle over the fruit. Fold the pastry over, but don't close it up completely.

Place the pastries in a pot and stand it on a tripod over hot coals. Create a Dutch oven by popping the lid on and placing some coals on top of it. Bake for 15 to 20 minutes or until done, but be careful you don't burn the bottom of the pastry.

STONED OLIVES ★ PARTNERS

Apple TART

THIS IS BERTUS'S MOM'S RECIPE, AND POSSIBLY THE BEST BAKED APPLE TART I'VE EVER TASTED. I ALSO HAVE A BETTER UNDERSTANDING OF WHERE CHEF BERTUS'S LOVE FOR GOOD FOOD COMES FROM. SERVE IT WITH WHIPPED CREAM OR HOME-MADE WARM CUSTARD . . . OR BOTH. THANK YOU, TANNIE HETTA . . . I THINK I LOVE YOU!

First up, cream the butter and sugar in a mixing bowl. Add the eggs and milk and mix thoroughly (until your arms start hurting). Put to one side. Sieve the flour, baking powder and salt together. Fold the dry ingredients into the creamed butter and sugar. Grease a flat-bottomed potjie and pour in the mixture. Give the batter bowl to your kid (after you've licked out half yourself). Layer the apples on top of the batter (multiple layers is fine) and bake on a grid over medium hot coals (180°C) until golden brown. (Check page 165 for help on coal temperatures.)

★ VANILLA SYRUP

Scrape the vanilla pod with a knife and add it to the cream and sugar. Whack everything into a pot and put it on medium hot coals. Simmer for 10 minutes and the minute the tart comes off the coals, pour the hot sauce over it and let your friends dig in.

YOU'LL NEED:
- 60 g butter
- 140 g sugar
- 3 eggs
- 70 ml milk
- 130 g flour
- 10 g baking powder
- a pinch of salt
- 8-10 apples – peeled, cored and cut into wedges

VANILLA SYRUP:
- 1 vanilla pod – scraped
- 250 g cream
- 250 g sugar

29

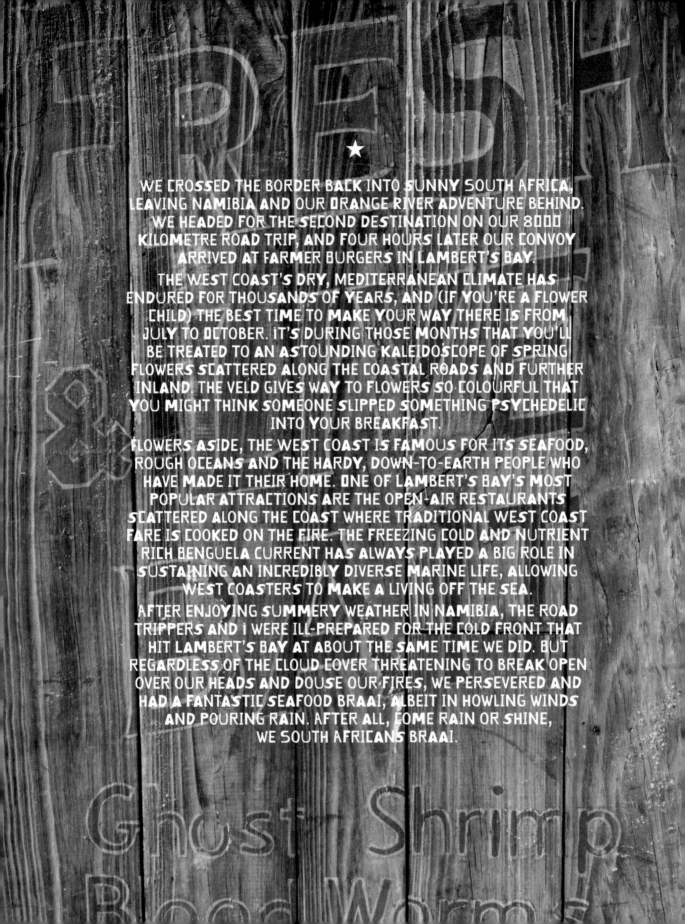

★

WE CROSSED THE BORDER BACK INTO SUNNY SOUTH AFRICA, LEAVING NAMIBIA AND OUR ORANGE RIVER ADVENTURE BEHIND. WE HEADED FOR THE SECOND DESTINATION ON OUR 8000 KILOMETRE ROAD TRIP, AND FOUR HOURS LATER OUR CONVOY ARRIVED AT FARMER BURGERS IN LAMBERT'S BAY.

THE WEST COAST'S DRY, MEDITERRANEAN CLIMATE HAS ENDURED FOR THOUSANDS OF YEARS, AND (IF YOU'RE A FLOWER CHILD) THE BEST TIME TO MAKE YOUR WAY THERE IS FROM JULY TO OCTOBER. IT'S DURING THOSE MONTHS THAT YOU'LL BE TREATED TO AN ASTOUNDING KALEIDOSCOPE OF SPRING FLOWERS SCATTERED ALONG THE COASTAL ROADS AND FURTHER INLAND. THE VELD GIVES WAY TO FLOWERS SO COLOURFUL THAT YOU MIGHT THINK SOMEONE SLIPPED SOMETHING PSYCHEDELIC INTO YOUR BREAKFAST.

FLOWERS ASIDE, THE WEST COAST IS FAMOUS FOR ITS SEAFOOD, ROUGH OCEANS AND THE HARDY, DOWN-TO-EARTH PEOPLE WHO HAVE MADE IT THEIR HOME. ONE OF LAMBERT'S BAY'S MOST POPULAR ATTRACTIONS ARE THE OPEN-AIR RESTAURANTS SCATTERED ALONG THE COAST WHERE TRADITIONAL WEST COAST FARE IS COOKED ON THE FIRE. THE FREEZING COLD AND NUTRIENT RICH BENGUELA CURRENT HAS ALWAYS PLAYED A BIG ROLE IN SUSTAINING AN INCREDIBLY DIVERSE MARINE LIFE, ALLOWING WEST COASTERS TO MAKE A LIVING OFF THE SEA.

AFTER ENJOYING SUMMERY WEATHER IN NAMIBIA, THE ROAD TRIPPERS AND I WERE ILL-PREPARED FOR THE COLD FRONT THAT HIT LAMBERT'S BAY AT ABOUT THE SAME TIME WE DID. BUT REGARDLESS OF THE CLOUD COVER THREATENING TO BREAK OPEN OVER OUR HEADS AND DOUSE OUR FIRES, WE PERSEVERED AND HAD A FANTASTIC SEAFOOD BRAAI, ALBEIT IN HOWLING WINDS AND POURING RAIN. AFTER ALL, COME RAIN OR SHINE, WE SOUTH AFRICANS BRAAI.

Our World Famous CRAB CAKES

ONLY SOLD HERE

muisbosskerm
LAMBERTSBAAI

Dressed Cray
WITH ASIAN SLAW

Get your hands on five live crayfish (not a problem if you're on the West Coast) and get ready to do the unthinkable, which is to kill them. My philosophy is that if you're going to eat it, you have to be able to kill it.

If you want to, you can put it in the freezer/cooler box filled with ice until it's immobile or no longer trying to crawl away from you. (Just make sure you don't end up freezing it – 30 to 60 minutes max should do the trick.) Then take the (now sleeping) crayfish and kill it with a sharp knife either by spiking it through the eyes in one quick movement, or through the chest wall from the underside.

CLEAN IT: Turn the crayfish on its back and stretch out the tail. Using a heavy knife, cut through the middle of the shell, from the tail to the soft abdomen and the harder body shell in between the legs right up to the head. Clean out the thin strip of the alimentary canal and pat dry.

Next, cut the crayfish open from the top to the bottom, straight down the middle (think butterfly effect). Baste with butter, lime juice and chopped chilli and then place, flesh side down, on a braai grid over medium hot coals, for about 5 minutes. The crayfish flesh is opaque, but when you braai it, it turns white, and as soon as it does, take it off the braai and baste it one last time, then set aside to cool.

WHILE YOU'RE BRAAIING THE CRAYS, GET YOUR BUDDY TO MAKE THE ASIAN SLAW: Mix together all the slaw ingredients (except for the baby fennel, bean sprouts and sesame seeds). Make sure that you don't add too much mayonnaise – you want to dress the slaw lightly, not drench it.

Scoop the crayfish meat out of the shells but be careful not to break the shells because you're going to use them as bowls. Cut up the cray meat roughly and mix it with the Asian slaw. Drizzle with some of the dressing and toss the mixture thoroughly. Scoop it back into the crayfish shells, and sprinkle the fennel, bean sprouts and sesame seeds on top.

Serve with extra lemon slices and a bottle of ridiculously good dry white wine.

FOR THE SLAW:
- ¼ cabbage – finely shredded
- 1 red onion – finely chopped
- 2 carrots – shaved
- ¼ cucumber – julienned
- 1 chilli if very hot, or 2 if not so hot
- small handful of coriander – chopped
- small chunk of ginger – grated
- juice of 2 lemons
- 2 spring onions – sliced very thinly (lengthwise)
- 2 pinches of chopped mint
- 2 pinches of chopped parsley
- 3 tablespoons of good quality mayonnaise (if you know how to make your own mayo, go for it, but if you don't, buy a decent one)
- 2 cloves of garlic – very (very) thinly sliced
- shaved baby fennel
- bean sprouts
- sesame seeds

FOR THE DRESSING, MIX TOGETHER:
- a generous squeeze of lemon juice
- a splash of Kikkoman soya sauce
- a drizzle of honey
- a pinch of sea salt and cracked black pepper
- a sprinkle of toasted sesame seeds

CANNED SARDINES ON TOAST ARE USUALLY ONE OF THOSE 'END-OF-THE-MONTH' MEALS THAT YOU CAN STRETCH A LONG WAY TO FEED YOUR FAMILY. IT MIGHT SOUND LIKE POOR MAN'S FOOD, BUT BECAUSE IT'S SUCH A RICH FISH, THE HUMBLE SARDINE HAS LOADS OF HEALTH BENEFITS. MY ADVICE? KEEP IT SIMPLE TO ENJOY ITS NATURAL FLAVOUR.

SARDINES *On Toast*

ULTIMATE BRAAI RECIPE ★ JUSTIN BONELLO

GO TO YOUR LOCAL FISHMONGER AND GET YOUR HANDS ON ABOUT 12 FRESH SARDINES, BUT YOU SHOULD BRAAI AND EAT THEM ON THE SAME DAY. IF THE FISHMONGER HASN'T CLEANED THE FISH FOR YOU, DO IT YOURSELF:

STEP 1

Hold the sardines under a cold running tap, then rub the scales off with a butter knife (or just use your thumbnail).

2

If don't like staring your food in the eye, snap the heads off with your hands, but if you can, leave them on.

3

With a paring knife, slit the fish open from the belly down to the tail. Carefully scrape out any remaining innards and rinse under cold water again. Rub some coarse sea salt on the inside of the sardines.

Once you've cleaned the sardines, keep them in a cool spot while you make the marinade.

Mix everything together and then pour the marinade over the sardines and cover with cling wrap. Let the sardines rest in the marinade for a couple of hours in the fridge or cooler box, while you whip up a quick vinaigrette.

Next up, make the vinaigrette. Put all the ingredients into an old (but clean) jam jar, pop the lid on and shake it vigorously.

Place the marinated sardines in a sandwich grid and braai over medium coals for 5 minutes or until cooked through. Take off the heat and set aside.

Now you're almost ready to eat. Cut a fresh government loaf or ciabatta into thick slices, top with sardines and drizzle with vinaigrette.

Think of the bread as a plate: eat the fish off the bread with your hands (Portuguese style) then put it on to the braai grid to toast. The oil and flavour of the fish will have soaked into the bread, making for a really *lekker* toasty treat afterwards.

FOR THE MARINADE YOU'LL NEED:
- the juice and zest of a couple of lemons
- a couple of cloves of garlic – crushed and chopped
- a couple of pinches of fresh thyme – chopped
- a handful of dill – chopped
- salt and pepper to taste

DILL AND MUSTARD VINAIGRETTE:
- a couple of splashes of white wine vinegar
- ¼ onion – finely chopped
- a small handful of dill – chopped
- salt and pepper to taste
- a dollop of wholegrain mustard
- juice and zest of 1 lemon
- a small glug of olive oil
- a pinch of sugar

Thai Fishcakes
IN BANANA LEAVES

YOU DON'T NEED TO GO TO THAILAND TO EXPERIENCE THAI FLAVOURS AND THESE FISHCAKES ARE GREAT TO ADD TO YOUR SUMMERTIME BRAAI MENU FOR THOSE LESS HUNGRY DAYS.

First up, finely chop the fish and put it in a mixing bowl. Take a mortar and pestle and bash up the garlic, ginger, lime juice and zest, basil, chilli and mint and mix it in with the fish. Add the chopped spring onion and a splash of fish sauce and mix together thoroughly until you have a fish patty mix. Cover and let the flavours infuse for about half an hour.

Next, take some banana leaves (yes, the ones you just cut from your neighbour's garden) and wash them thoroughly. Cut them into 10 x 10 cm squares. Shape golf ball size scoops of the fish mixture into patties and place each on a banana leaf, then top it with a leaf of basil. Fold the edges of the banana leaf over the fish cake and secure it with toothpicks.

Braai over medium coals for about 3 minutes a side or until the fish is cooked through and the banana leaves are slightly charred on the outside.

YOU'LL NEED:
- about ½ kg of firm white fish fillets – deboned
- 2 cloves of garlic – crushed and chopped
- a large chunk of ginger – peeled and grated
- zest and juice of 2 limes
- a large handful of fresh basil
- 1 chilli – seeds removed and chopped
- a small handful of fresh mint – chopped
- 4 spring onions – finely chopped
- a splash of fish sauce

ULTIMATE BRAAI RECIPE
JUSTIN BONELLO

Mussel Pots

FROM THE WEST COAST, WE MADE OUR WAY TO SCARBOROUGH, A SLEEPY SEASIDE TOWN ABOUT 40 MINUTES FROM CAPE TOWN (DEPENDING ON WHO'S DRIVING). SCARBOROUGH IS SURROUNDED BY MOUNTAINS, NATURE RESERVES AND THE OCEAN AND IS A HAVEN FOR PEOPLE WHO ENJOY A MORE SLOW-PACED LIFESTYLE: SURFERS, FREE-THINKERS AND, OF COURSE, OUR EVER-LOVABLE HIPPIE CROWD. THIS IDYLLIC TOWN IS JUST FAR ENOUGH FROM THE MOTHER CITY TO KEEP THE MAJORITY OF CAPETONIANS FROM MOVING HERE PERMANENTLY, BUT IT'S CLOSE ENOUGH FOR THE PERFECT WEEKEND GETAWAY. ADDING TO THE QUIET BEAUTY OF SCARBOROUGH IS THE FACT THAT ONLY A SMALL HANDFUL OF LUCKY RESIDENTS GET TO CALL IT HOME. WAY BACK IN 1996 IT WAS DECLARED A CONSERVATION AREA IN AN EFFORT TO PROTECT IT FROM ANY FUTURE ENVIRONMENTAL WRONGDOERS AND TO TRY TO REVERSE THE DAMAGE OF THE PAST. THIS IS DEFINITELY MY KIND OF PLACE – WHICH I ADMIT MIGHT MAKE ME A BIT OF HIPPIE.

THE REASON I BROUGHT THE ROAD TRIPPERS TO SCARBOROUGH WAS BECAUSE IT'S ONE OF MY SECRET SPOTS TO GET CRAYFISH (WHEN IN SEASON) AND MUSSELS (WHENEVER I FEEL LIKE IT). THEY ARRIVED AND WERE HANDED FISHING PERMITS AND INSTRUCTIONS ON HOW TO HARVEST MUSSELS AND OFF THEY WENT. THE PLAN? TO MAKE THE PERFECT MUSSEL POT USING FRESHLY PICKED MUSSELS AND THEIR IMAGINATIONS. THESE WERE TWO OF THE BEST.

POWER POT ★

First, heat up a potjie, chuck the mussels in and add a couple of splashes of dry white wine (and a sip for yourself to check that it's good enough for the mussels). Pop the lid on and let the mussels steam until they open up. Throw away the mussels that didn't open – unless the thought of seafood poisoning appeals to you (weirdo). Clean the mussels by pulling out the beards.

Next, heat up another potjie (over medium coals) and add a knob of butter and a splash of olive oil (this will prevent the butter from burning). Add the chopped onion and sauté. When the onion is soft, add the garlic, tomato and fish spice. Simmer for a couple of minutes then put in the mussels and salt and pepper to taste. While the potjie's simmering, whip up a lemon and chilli butter – simply squeeze a lemon into a couple of knobs of butter, add the chopped chilli and mash it up with a fork. Ladle the mussels into serving bowls and finish off by letting a knob of chilli butter melt over the top. Nice.

PS: Sindi and Lethu had never harvested or cooked mussels before. In fact, on the day they looked at me and asked me where the mussels were. They were standing on top of them. Lesson? If they could pull off a delicious mussel pot without any prior experience, so can you.

YOU'LL NEED:
- a couple of big handfuls of fresh mussels
- a couple of glugs of dry white wine
- a big knob of butter
- a splash of olive oil
- 1 onion – chopped
- 3 cloves of garlic – crushed and chopped
- 2 ½ to 3 tomatoes – chopped
- a couple of pinches of fish spice (that's a combination of dried basil, dill, garlic powder, onion powder, dried oregano and dried lemon zest)
- salt and pepper
- lemon
- extra butter
- 1 or 2 red chillies – chopped (use more if you want it hotter)

COOKING SOUL BROTHERS

★ SOUL POT

First up, put the mussels in a potjie, add a generous splash of white wine, pop the lid on, let them steam until they open and then pull out the beards . . . just like Gal Power did.

In a separate potjie, melt the butter, add the chopped red onion, sliced fennel and fennel seeds and cook until soft. Add the chopped tomatoes, white wine vinegar, salt and pepper and the cleaned mussels and simmer for a couple of minutes to allow the flavours to infuse and develop. Just before they're done, add the cream and the lemon juice and stir the potjie thoroughly. Leave it for about a minute, remove from the heat, ladle into bowls and top with fresh coriander and dill. Squeeze some more fresh lemon over the top and serve. Fresh.

YOU'LL NEED:
- a couple of handfuls of mussels
- ½ cup of dry white wine
- a knob of butter
- ½ red onion – chopped
- 1 fennel bulb – finely sliced
- about a tablespoon of fennel seeds
- 1 can whole peeled tomatoes – chopped
- a splash of white wine vinegar
- salt and cracked black pepper
- ½ cup of cream
- juice of ½ lemon
- a small handful of fresh coriander
  – roughly chopped
- a couple of pinches of dill
  – chopped

MUSSEL TIP: IF YOU HARVEST YOUR OWN MUSSELS AND WANT TO GET RID OF ALL THE SAND AND GRIT THEY SOMETIMES COME ALONG WITH, SOAK THEM IN FRESH SEAWATER FOR A COUPLE OF HOURS AND THEY'LL SPIT OUT THE SAND. EASY.

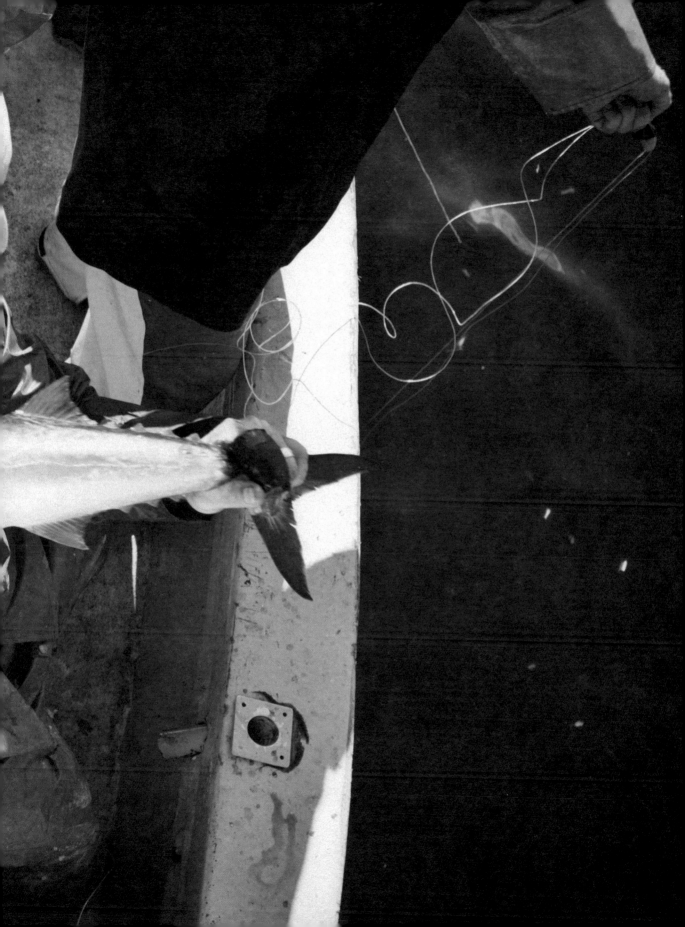

THE KRAAIFONTEIN
Crocodile

In New Zealand it's called a barracouta, scientists call it *Thyrsites atun* and here in South Africa we simply call it snoek (the distant cousin of the snake mackerel). If the Springbok is our rugby team's emblem and the Protea our national flower then, based on its popularity, snoek should be South Africa's national fish (but it's not, the galjoen is). If you ever have the misfortune to emigrate, snoek will probably be one of the things you'll miss most – that and Mrs Ball's chutney.

I love snoek, and many years ago I had my first taste of catching my own with my mate Gareth Beaumont, aka 'The Fish Assassin'.

The proper way to catch snoek is with your bare hands using a method called hand lining. If you think you know what hand lining is, you're probably right: What you do is put on a *vingerlappie* (it looks like one of those rubber thimbles your gran uses for needlework), grab a line and a chunk of bait and off you go.

On the day I came face to face with my very first snoek I finally understood why many refer to it as the *Kraaifontein Crocodile*.

Let me explain. Once the snoek locks its jaws on to your bait and you pull it out, you'd better watch out for its teeth. This is not the kind of fish that will lie on its back and let you tickle its belly. The minute you pull it out of the water and on to the boat, you'll probably think that it wants to eat you (play *Jaws* type music here). The snoek's razor sharp teeth will snap at you until the bitter end.

AN EYE FOR AN EYE... If you actually go out on a boat to catch your own snoek – well done! If you end up getting bitten, don't say I didn't warn you! Unfortunately for you, because of the anticoagulant on their teeth, you'll probably now bleed to death, so start saying your goodbyes. Okay, okay . . . just kidding. If a snoek manages to sink its teeth into you, take one of its eyeballs, slit it and squeeze the gel on to the bite to stop the bleeding. Yes. Seriously!

48

VLEKKING

Down in the Cape, gutting and butterflying a fish is called *vlekking*. First, cut the snoek open along the backbone, from the tail to the head. Remove the entrails and head and rinse the body under running water. Then make an incision down the centre of each fillet, but be careful not to cut through the skin. This increases the surface area of the fish and you will be left with two butterflied halves. Rub some salt on to the fish and hang it outside for about 20 minutes. Rinse it again and pat dry. Let it hang outside in the wind until it's tacky.

Snoek

WITH SPICY CHIMICHURRI

CHIMICHURRI IS A SPICY SALSA, POPULAR IN ARGENTINA. IT'S GREAT WITH FISH AND CHICKEN, AND IF YOU'RE LIKE ME AND YOU LIKE IT VERY SPICY, ADD EXTRA CHILLIES.

Toss the red pepper on the braai and turn until all sides are completely charred and blackened. Wrap it in cling film immediately and leave it to sweat for a minute. Pull cling film off to remove blackened skin, rinse the pepper under cold water and then chop it finely. Add the chopped parsley, origanum, onion, chilli, thyme, paprika, cumin, garlic and crushed bay leaves and mix it all together. Pour in a glug of olive oil and two glugs of red wine vinegar. Set the chimichurri aside while you vlek the snoek (check out page 49).

As soon as the snoek is ready, put it on a braai grid (the sandwich kind), close and braai the skin side for a couple of minutes. Then flip the grid over and braai the flesh side for a few minutes before flipping it over again so that the snoek is back on its skin side. Pack the flesh side liberally with chimichurri. Braai for no longer than 10 to 20 minutes and just before the snoek is done, brush with honey and lemon, braai for another minute and remove from the coals. Don't overcook it – it becomes dry in a heartbeat.

YOU'LL NEED:
- 1 red pepper
- 2 handfuls of parsley – chopped
- a small handful of fresh origanum – chopped
- ½ red onion
- a couple of chillies
- a couple of sprigs of thyme
- a couple of pinches of paprika
- a couple of pinches of cumin
- a couple of garlic cloves – chopped
- 2 dried bay leaves – crushed
- a couple of generous glugs of olive oil
- 2 glugs of red wine vinegar
- 1 snoek – vlekked
- honey
- the juice of a lemon

SERVE WITH BASHED HERB POTATO SALAD (PAGE 54) AND PEAR AND WALNUT SALAD (PAGE 53).

Braai'd Pear, WALNUT AND Crème Fraiche SALAD

BERTUS BASSON CHEF BRAAI MASTER JUDGE

BERTUS BASSON IS ONE OF SOUTH AFRICA'S TOP CHEFS AND A CULINARY GENIUS IN HIS OWN RIGHT. WHAT I LOVE ABOUT HIM IS THAT HE'S DOWN TO EARTH AND KEEPS HIS RECIPES SIMPLE. THE RESULT? A MIND-BOGGLING, MOUTH-WATERING COMBINATION OF FLAVOURS THAT WILL KEEP A SMILE ON YOUR FACE LONG AFTER YOUR LAST BITE.

This salad is ideal for summertime. But if you want to make it into a meal, add chopped bacon and replace the crème fraiche with blue cheese. Usually I wouldn't bother with exact quantities, just feeling my way, but this is Bertus's recipe, so I'm giving it to you exactly how he gave it to me. If you don't like it you can complain to him. (Just kidding! It's delicious.)

Dress the sliced pears with honey, olive oil and some salt and pepper, then grill them on medium to hot coals for 3 to 4 minutes on each side. Remove them from the heat and drizzle with honey. Next, assemble the lettuce and onion, top with the chargrilled pears, shavings of Parmesan cheese, roasted walnuts and dollops of crème fraiche. Season with salt and pepper and finish with the home-made croutons and a drizzle of olive oil, sprinklings of lemon zest and a good squeeze of lemon juice.

★ HOME-MADE CROUTONS

These are really easy to make and are great for adding crunch and flavour to salads and soups. This is all you need to do. Take a loaf of bread, preferably a couple of days old. Cut it into cubes and put them in a bowl. Drizzle generously with olive oil and, using your hands, toss around until all the bread is covered, but not soaked through. Spread the bread cubes in a roasting pan and sprinkle with salt and pepper. Bake in a preheated oven at 200°C for about 10 minutes or until toasted, turning the croutons over at half time.

For different varieties of crouton, play around and season with garlic and chilli, lemongrass, rosemary or sage . . . you get the idea, use whatever tickles your fancy.

GET YOUR FIRE STARTED, THEN GO PREP THE FOLLOWING:

- 2 pears – peeled and sliced width-wise into 1 cm thick slices (keep the slices in lemon water to prevent them from going brown)
- 45 ml honey
- 45 ml olive oil
- salt and pepper
- 100 g lettuce leaves of your choice
- 40 g red onion – thinly sliced
- Parmesan cheese shavings
- 60 g walnuts – roasted
- crème fraiche
- home-made croutons
- lemon juice and olive oil for dressing
- zest and juice of another lemon (keep both separate)

BASHED HERB
& Roasted Potato
SALAD

SOMETIMES THE SIMPLE THINGS IN LIFE PUT A SMILE ON MY FACE. A DECENT CUP OF COFFEE IN THE MORNING. A FISH THAT FINALLY TAKES MY BAIT. PLAYING IN THE GARDEN WITH MY LIGHTIE. A BEAUTIFUL SUNSET AFTER A LONG DAY . . . AND (REALLY) GOOD POTATO SALAD.

Parboil the baby potatoes, cut them in half and put them in a roasting tin along with the chopped garlic. Drizzle with olive oil, coarse sea salt and a generous crack of black pepper, cover with foil and whack on to a medium to hot fire. Once your potatoes are roasted (soft on the inside, crispy on the outside) let them cool down. In the meantime, grab your mortar and pestle, add all the herbs and a drizzle of olive oil and bash them to release all the flavours. Toss the herbs, grated Parmesan and a glug of white balsamic vinegar with the (now cooled) potatoes. Sprinkle with toasted sesame seeds (as much as you like) and tuck in.

PS: One of my favourite ways to roast potatoes these days is in duck fat. If you can find some, use it instead of olive oil . . . you'll never look back.

YOU'LL NEED:
- a couple of handfuls of baby potatoes
- 2-3 cloves of garlic – crushed and chopped
- a glug of olive oil
- coarse sea salt and black pepper
- a large handful of rocket
- a handful of basil
- a handful of parsley
- about 1 cup of grated Parmesan
- a generous glug of white balsamic vinegar
- a tablespoon of toasted sesame seeds

HAVE THIS WITH SNOEK (PAGE 50), CAJUN CALAMARI (PAGE 80) OR JUST BY ITSELF AS A LEFTOVER BREAKFAST THE NEXT MORNING (YOU KNOW WHAT I'M TALKING ABOUT).

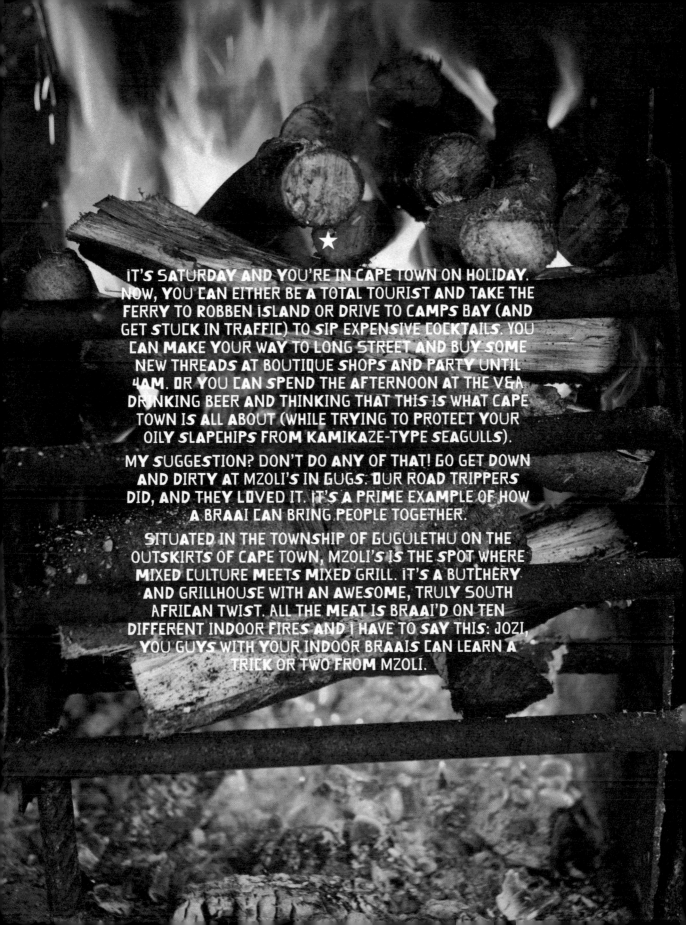

IT'S SATURDAY AND YOU'RE IN CAPE TOWN ON HOLIDAY. NOW, YOU CAN EITHER BE A TOTAL TOURIST AND TAKE THE FERRY TO ROBBEN ISLAND OR DRIVE TO CAMPS BAY (AND GET STUCK IN TRAFFIC) TO SIP EXPENSIVE COCKTAILS. YOU CAN MAKE YOUR WAY TO LONG STREET AND BUY SOME NEW THREADS AT BOUTIQUE SHOPS AND PARTY UNTIL 4AM. OR YOU CAN SPEND THE AFTERNOON AT THE V&A DRINKING BEER AND THINKING THAT THIS IS WHAT CAPE TOWN IS ALL ABOUT (WHILE TRYING TO PROTECT YOUR OILY SLAPCHIPS FROM KAMIKAZE-TYPE SEAGULLS).

MY SUGGESTION? DON'T DO ANY OF THAT! GO GET DOWN AND DIRTY AT MZOLI'S IN GUGS. OUR ROAD TRIPPERS DID, AND THEY LOVED IT. IT'S A PRIME EXAMPLE OF HOW A BRAAI CAN BRING PEOPLE TOGETHER.

SITUATED IN THE TOWNSHIP OF GUGULETHU ON THE OUTSKIRTS OF CAPE TOWN, MZOLI'S IS THE SPOT WHERE MIXED CULTURE MEETS MIXED GRILL. IT'S A BUTCHERY AND GRILLHOUSE WITH AN AWESOME, TRULY SOUTH AFRICAN TWIST. ALL THE MEAT IS BRAAI'D ON TEN DIFFERENT INDOOR FIRES AND I HAVE TO SAY THIS: JOZI, YOU GUYS WITH YOUR INDOOR BRAAIS CAN LEARN A TRICK OR TWO FROM MZOLI.

MZOLI
TSHISA

DON'T JUST BUY A DRINK. BUY A CASE

* DON'T ORDER ONE CHOP. ORDER A PLATTER WITH PAP & CHAKALAKA.

NEVER EVER ASK FOR THE RECIPE FOR MZOLIS SAUCE. IT'S A SECRET

I'S

MZOLI'S MEAT

U M B

CAPE TOWN

NYAMA!

EAT WITH YOUR HANDS

PARTY WITH THE LOCALS

AND BEFORE YOU KNOW IT YOUR HEAD (AND BODY) WILL BE MOVING TO THE BEAT OF DEEP HOUSE AND KWAITO AND YOUR QUART OF BEER WILL BE FOAMING AT THE MOUTH.

PS TAKE A TAXI OR GET A DESIGNATED DRIVER!

WE LEFT THE MOTHER CITY AND THE LIFE OF ABUNDANCE BEHIND AND TRAVELLED INTO THE KAROO. THE THING ABOUT THIS BARREN LANDSCAPE IS THAT IF YOU RACE PAST IT ON THE N1 (ON YOUR WAY TO JOHANNESBURG OR CAPE TOWN) YOU'LL NEVER GET TO KNOW ITS HEARTBEAT, ITS PEOPLE OR WHAT MAKES THEM TICK. I COULD TELL YOU ABOUT THE BROAD PLAINS THAT ROLL AWAY TOWARDS DISTANT BLUE MOUNTAINS AND ENDLESS HORIZONS AND ABOUT THE INCREDIBLE HOSPITALITY OF THE PEOPLE WHO LIVE THERE. BUT I WON'T. YOU SHOULD PACK YOUR CAR, TRAVEL DEEP INTO THE ARID LANDSCAPES AND SET UP CAMP. ONLY THEN WILL YOU UNDERSTAND THE MAGIC, WHERE THE ONLY NOISE YOU'LL HEAR IS THE SOUND OF YOUR OWN THOUGHTS AND THE CRACKLING OF YOUR BRAAI FIRE. THIS IS THE KIND OF SPACE THAT REALLY KICKS MY GOOSE.

IF YOU MANAGE TO GET YOUR HANDS ON A WHOLE LAMB, THIS IS WHAT YOU CAN DO WITH IT TO MAKE SURE NONE OF IT GOES TO WASTE:

HEAD
BLOWTORCH, BOIL AND THEN BRAAI SMILEYS
THE SWEET MEAT OF THE CHEEKS IS GREAT

NECK
PERFECT FOR POTJIE KOS. DON'T BRAAI!

LOIN
LOIN CHOPS: THICK CUT, RUB, BRAAI
LOIN ROAST: MARINATE OVERNIGHT AND BRAAI SLOWLY

KAROO LAMB CUTS
U M B
THE ULTIMATE BRAAI MASTER

RACK
WHOLE RACK: MARINATE OVERNIGHT AND BRAAI FOR A COUPLE OF HOURS
•••••••••••••••••• RIB CHOPS: RUB AND BRAAI

SIRLOIN
WHOLE: KEEP WHOLE, MARINATE OVERNIGHT, BRAAI SLOWLY
STEAKS: MARINATE, BRAAI — KEEP MEDIUM RARE
KEBABS: CUBE, MARINATE OVERNIGHT, BRAAI — KEEP MEDIUM RARE
(CHECK OUT KAROO CANAPÉS, OVERLEAF)

★ SHOULDER ★
SQUARE CUT SHOULDER: MARINATE OVERNIGHT AND BRAAI SLOWLY • ARM CHOP: MARINATE AND BRAAI
SHOULDER BLADE CHOP: THICK CUTS, RUB, BRAAI • SHOULDER ROLL: DEBONE SHOULDER, MARINATE OR RUB, STUFF AND ROLL

BREAST
SPARERIBS: SMOKE AND BRAAI SLOWLY WITH BASTING SAUCE ★ RIBLETS: SMOKE AND BRAAI SLOWLY
ROLLED BREAST: RUB, STUFF AND THEN SPIT BRAAI SLOWLY OR ROAST IN OVEN ★ BURGERS: DEBONE AND MINCE TO MAKE BRAAI PATTIES

SHANK
LAMB SHANKS: POTJIE OR SLOW ROAST
STEW MEAT: POTJIE, STEWS OR SOUPS

LEG
WHOLE: MARINATE AND BRAAI SLOWLY – MEDIUM
DEBONED: MARINATE AND BRAAI SLOWLY– MEDIUM

LIVER
BRAAI OR PANFRY OVER HOT COALS

KIDNEYS
BRAAI OR PANFRY OVER HOT COALS
CAN ALSO MAKE STEAK AND KIDNEY PIE

TRIPE&TROTTERS
CLEAN REALLY WELL AND THEN MAKE CURRIED OFFAL
(OR JUST GIVE IT TO YOUR DOGS FOR A TREAT)

TAILS
SALT, PEPPER, BRAAI. GREAT SNACK

KAROO *canapés*

★

LAMB LIVER ON FIRE-BAKED BRUSCHETTA

FIRE-BAKED BRUSCHETTA:
First, take a bowl and dissolve the yeast in the warm water to activate it. Mix all the dry ingredients together, then pour the yeasty water into the flour. Mix and knead well. Proof until double in size (in other words, cover it with a tea towel and leave it in a warm spot to rise), then knock it down and shape the bread. Proof it again until it doubles in size, knock it down again and form into a ciabatta shape. Bake it on a grid over medium coals (150-160°C) until golden brown.

LAMB LIVER:
Clean the liver and cut it into slices about 1 cm thick. Heat a pan over medium hot coals, add a splash of oil and fry the liver. Just before it's cooked (no longer than 5 minutes) season with salt and black pepper to taste.

CUCUMBER PICKLE:
Pour the sugar, water and white wine vinegar into a small potjie, place it on the heat and bring to a simmer. Remove from the heat, allow the pickling juice to cool and then add the cucumber.

FIRE-BAKED BRUSCHETTA:
• 10 g dried yeast or 40 g fresh yeast
• 750 ml warm water
• 1 kg flour
• 30 g salt
• 30 g sugar

LAMB LIVER:
• 1 lamb liver
• olive oil
• salt and pepper
• a couple of dates – thinly sliced

CUCUMBER PICKLE:
• 50 g sugar
• 100 ml water
• 50 ml white wine vinegar
• a handful of finely julienned cucumber

★

TO SERVE, SLICE THE BRUSCHETTA, TOP WITH LIVER, SLICED DATES AND CUCUMBER RELISH.

KAROO CANAPÉS

★ LAMB ON LAMB SKEWERS

YOU'LL NEED:
- 1 lamb fillet and 1 lamb rump – cut into cubes
- the thinnest lamb ribs you can get your hands on
- cumin
- thyme
- coriander
- salt and pepper
- a couple of beetroot – peeled
- olive oil and lemon juice for basting

Mix together equal quantities of cumin, thyme, coriander, salt and pepper and rub the spice into the lamb cubes then set them aside. (If you have any lamb rub left over, put it in an airtight container and store it in your spice rack.) Bring a pot of water to the boil, add the peeled beetroot and let it cook for about 15 minutes or until al dente. Remove from the heat, pour off the water and allow to cool.

Clean the bones of the lamb ribs by scraping the meat off with a sharp knife. (The meat off the bones was used for a broth – you can do the same.) Skewer the lamb cubes on to the rib bones, with sliced beetroot between each cube of meat. Now you're going to make a zesty reduction before you braai the skewers.

MINTY REDUCTION
Warm up some olive oil in a saucepan then fry a couple of cloves of chopped garlic until soft. Add a few splashes of balsamic vinegar and a small handful of chopped mint, stir it and simmer until it reduces by half.

Braai the lamb skewers on medium to hot coals for about 5 minutes until medium rare, basting frequently with olive oil and lemon juice. Serve with the reduction drizzled over the top.

★
POTATO SCALLOPS WITH SHIMEJI MUSHROOMS AND LAMB

YOU'LL NEED:
- a couple of medium-sized potatoes – peeled
- salted butter
- 1 onion – chopped
- a couple of cloves of garlic – crushed and chopped
- a handful of Shimeji mushrooms
- lamb fillet and rump – cut into strips
- a splash of cream
- ½ cup of cream cheese
- ½ cup of crème fraiche
- a small handful of fresh coriander – chopped
- a couple of chillies – deseeded and chopped

Cut the potatoes into slices roughly 1 cm thick then pop them on to the grid and braai until crispy on the outside. Remove from the heat, baste with salted butter and keep warm.

Next, fry the chopped onion, garlic and mushrooms in a pan over hot coals. When cooked remove from the pan and set aside. In the same pan, fry the lamb strips and as soon as they have caramelised on the outside (but still rare on the inside) add a splash of cream, and the mushroom mix. When the cream has warmed through, take it off the heat. The lamb should be medium rare and not cooked to death or it will become tough.

Scoop the lamb on to the potato scallops. Mix together the cream cheese, crème fraiche, coriander and chilli and drizzle this creamy sauce over the lamb.

★

MATJIESFONTEIN, LIKE ANY OTHER KAROO TOWN, TELLS AN
INTERESTING STORY, BUT THIS ONE IS MORE SUCCESSFUL THAN
MOST. THE STORY STARTS WA-AAAY BACK IN 1877 WHEN A YOUNG
SCOTSMAN, JAMES DOUGLAS LOGAN, WAS MAKING HIS MERRY
WAY TO AUSTRALIA BY SHIP BUT ENDED UP LEAVING IT IN SIMON'S
TOWN AND BEGAN WORKING ON THE RAILWAYS. LIKE ANY 20-YEAR-
OLD, JAMES HAD TO WORK HIS WAY UP IN LIFE, BUT EVENTUALLY
HE BECAME THE DISTRICT SUPERINTENDENT OF THE TOUWS RIVER/
PRINCE ALBERT ROAD SECTION OF THE RAILWAY. HE FELL IN LOVE WITH
THE KAROO LANDSCAPES AND, LIKE MANY OTHER EXPLORERS OF
THE TIME, DECIDED THAT THIS WAS WHERE HE WAS GOING TO MAKE
HIS FORTUNE. FIRST HE BOUGHT 2998 HECTARES OF FARMLAND,
BUILT A HOMESTEAD AND PLANTED THOUSANDS OF EUCALYPTUS
TREES. AFTER SOME TIME, HE BOUGHT ANOTHER 5139 HECTARES
AND DEVELOPED MATJIESFONTEIN.

NOW OLD JAMES (WHO I'M GUESSING WAS EITHER A HEAVY
SMOKER OR JUST HAD SOME BAD LUCK) SUFFERED FROM A WEAK
CHEST, AND WHEN HE BUILT MATJIESFONTEIN IT BECAME A VERY
SUCCESSFUL HEALTH RESORT BECAUSE OF ITS DRY AIR. BUT THEN
CAME THE ANGLO-BOER WAR AND MATJIESFONTEIN BECAME THE
HEADQUARTERS OF THE CAPE COMMAND AND NOT LONG AFTERWARDS
IT WAS TURNED INTO A MAKESHIFT MILITARY HOSPITAL. AFTER
LOGAN'S DEATH IN 1920, MATJIESFONTEIN WAS PASSED DOWN
TO HIS SON AND LATER TO HIS SON-IN-LAW. IN 1969 (NOTHING TO
DO WITH THE BRIAN ADAMS SONG) MATJIESFONTEIN WAS SOLD
AND RESTORED TO ITS FORMER VICTORIAN BEAUTY AND TODAY
IT'S A POPULAR GETAWAY SPOT FOR ANYONE WHO LIKES A BIT
OF OLD CHARM, EVEN THOUGH IT'S ONE OF THE MOST
HAUNTED PLACES IN SOUTH AFRICA.

BRAAI'D *Lamb Roll*

I THINK THIS RECIPE IS THE EPITOME OF A GOOD SUNDAY AFTERNOON MEAL. LEG OF LAMB USED TO BE MY FAVOURITE, BUT AFTER TASTING A LAMB ROLL, I'VE CHANGED MY MIND. MAKE SURE YOU INVITE LOADS OF DESERVING FRIENDS (THE KIND WHO WILL ARRIVE WITH BOTTLES AND BOTTLES OF SERIOUSLY GOOD WINE).

First up, mush together the butter, anchovies, garlic and rosemary, then place the lamb loin on top of the *lieslap*. Rub the flavoured butter all over the loin – be generous! If the loin is bigger than the one Greg and Karl used, make more butter. Once the lamb loin has been buttered to your satisfaction, roll it up inside the *lieslap* and secure with butcher's string, leaving about two finger spaces between each knot.

BASTING SAUCE: Mix together a couple of glugs of olive oil, the juice of 2 oranges and 2 lemons, about a cup of white wine, a couple of pinches of coarse sea salt and black pepper. Put the lamb roll on to a slow spit and let it braai slowly for approximately 2 hours, basting regularly. After 2 hours, take the lamb off the heat, sprinkle with some coarse sea salt and let the meat rest for a couple of minutes. Add more coals to the fire to bring the temperature up to a high heat, then put the lamb roll back on to the spit. Let it braai for another 15 minutes or until the outside is golden and crispy. Use a meat thermometer to check if the lamb has been cooked to your liking.

GREEN PAP: Pour the water into a large potjie over medium to hot coals. Add a decent pinch of salt, put the lid on and bring to the boil. Slowly pour the maize meal into the potjie – you want it to form a pyramid in the centre of the potjie. Without stirring, put the lid back on, scrape away some of the coals to reduce the heat and let the pap simmer for about 5 minutes. Remove the lid and, using a fork, stir the pap until it's crumbly, then cover it again. Simmer on a low heat for about an hour. Chop the herbs and spring onions and stir them into the pap just before serving.

CREAMY RED WINE REDUCTION: Heat a saucepan over medium coals, then add the cream, red wine, beef stock and couple of pinches of rosemary and thyme. Let it simmer for about 20 minutes or until the sauce has reduced by half.

TO SERVE: Cut the lamb roll into slices about 2 cm thick. Serve on top of the green pap and drizzle with the red wine reduction. Open a bottle of seriously good wine and eat and *kuier* with your friends until the sun goes down.

YOU'LL NEED:
(about 2 hours cooking time)

- about 250 g (half a block) of butter
- about 8 anchovies
- a couple of cloves of garlic – crushed and chopped
- a couple of sprigs of rosemary – finely chopped
- 1 whole lamb loin – deboned
- 1 *lieslap* (that's the skin on the outside of the flank)
- olive oil
- juice of 2 oranges
- juice of 2 lemons
- about 1 cup of white wine
- coarse sea salt and black pepper

GREEN PAP:
(about 60 minutes)

- 7 cups of water
- a generous pinch of salt
- 4 cups of maize meal
- a handful of fresh parsley
- a handful of spring onions
- a small handful of mint

RED WINE REDUCTION:
(about 20 minutes)

- 1 cup of cream
- 1 cup of red wine
- a splash of beef stock
- sprigs of rosemary and thyme

Greek Style
BRAAI'D LAMB

IF YOU'VE GOT MY FIRST BOOK, YOU'LL KNOW THAT I'VE ALREADY DONE A GREEK-STYLE LAMB, BUT I HAVE TO GIVE YOU MARTHINUS'S RECIPE. I'LL EVEN ADMIT THAT IT MIGHT BE BETTER THAN MINE! THIS IS SERIOUSLY DELICIOUS AND REALLY EASY TO MAKE.

YOU'LL NEED:
- 500 ml Bulgarian yoghurt
- 6 cloves of garlic – crushed and finely chopped
- juice of 3 lemons
- a small handful of rosemary – finely chopped
- a couple of pinches of smoked paprika
- salt and cracked black pepper
- 1 deboned leg of lamb (about 2.5 kg)

YOU'LL NEED:
- 4 brown anchovies
- a drizzle of olive oil
- a clove of garlic
- a generous squeeze of lemon juice (about ½ lemon)

First up, mix together the yoghurt, garlic, lemon juice, rosemary, smoked paprika, salt and black pepper. Then think of your favourite horror movie character, take a sharp knife and stab some holes into the lamb. Go wash the blood off your hands, then rub the yoghurt marinade all over the leg. Put it in a bowl, cover with cling wrap and hide the evidence in the fridge for two days. During that time, the cultures in this yoghurt-based marinade will break down the protein, which means that once you've cooked the lamb, it will be the most tender you've ever eaten.

Two days later, when your friends arrive, start your fire. Once you have medium coals, the lamb is ready for its final execution. Braai for about half an hour, basting every now and then with the leftover marinade. You want the lamb to caramelise on the outside, and be cooked (but still pink) on the inside. When done, remove from the heat, put the lamb aside to rest and rustle up a quick vinaigrette, which will offset the fattiness of the meat.

If you have a blender handy (which you would if you were at home . . . or if you're a chef) blitz all the ingredients until fine. If you're more like me and find yourself in the great outdoors, just wing it and use a mortar and pestle to mung the anchovies, garlic, lemon juice and olive oil.

Carve the lamb, drizzle with the vinaigrette and serve with whatever tickles your fancy.

RECESSION *Pudding*

I LOVE THIS RECIPE BECAUSE TO ME IT EPITOMISES THE KAROO LIFESTYLE WHERE NOTHING IS WASTED. RONEL FIRST MADE THIS AT THE HEIGHT OF THE RECESSION USING WHATEVER BITS AND BOBS SHE COULD FIND IN HER HOUSE. SOMETIMES I THINK THAT'S HOW THE BEST RECIPES COME TO BE. THIS IS HER REFINED VERSION.

STONED OLIVES · PARTNERS

First, take a flat-bottomed potjie and place it on a tripod or balance it on two bricks over the coals. Pour the milk in and let it heat up but don't let it boil. Cut the crust off the top of the bread loaf, scoop out the insides and keep the crust for later. Put the insides into a blender and blitz until you have breadcrumbs. Remove the warm (not boiling) milk from the fire, add 2 cups of breadcrumbs and set aside until the milk has cooled down and the bread crumbs have swollen. (Another great thing about this recipe is that you don't need to add baking powder or yeast because it's already in the bread.) Next, combine the three eggs and the sugar and whisk until creamy, then pour into the cooled bread and milk mixture. Mix well and set the potjie aside.

Now you're going to make the topping. Take the lonely discarded bread crust, put it into a blender and blitz until you have crumbs again. Mix the crumbs with brown sugar (to taste), the zest of one orange, a squeeze of orange juice and add the spices. Carefully sprinkle the topping over the bread pudding.

Put the potjie on a tripod over medium to low coals and place a couple of coals on top of the lid. If the temperature is too high the pudding will curdle, so rather bake it over a low heat for 2 hours. You can peek into the pot every now and then to check how it's doing.

About 10 minutes before serving, whip up a reduction. Do this by taking a fireproof saucepan, squeezing in the juice of the orange you used for the zest (and a second orange if needed). Cut the flesh of half the orange into segments, add it to the saucepan along with a squeeze of honey and reduce on medium to hot coals until syrupy. If the reduction becomes too sticky just squeeze in some more orange juice until it's syrupy again.

Remove the potjie from the heat, scoop the pudding out of the pot into serving bowls and drizzle with the orange reduction. *Lekker!*

★

YOU'LL NEED:
- 1 litre of milk
- 1 government loaf (white bread)
- 3 eggs
- 150-200 ml sugar
- brown sugar
- 1 orange
- 1 teaspoon of cinnamon
- 1 teaspoon of nutmeg
- a pinch of allspice
- honey

BLACKENED
Calamari

From the barren landscape of the Karoo we travelled to the ocean at Cape St Francis on the south-east coast. This coastal town first became famous in the 1960s in the surfing documentary *Endless Summers* when surfers Mike Hynson and Robert August surfed 'Bruce's Beauties' – an almost perfect wave that ran the entire length of the bay. What they didn't know was that this particular bay makes it prone to good swell generated by low-pressure systems that form between Antarctica and the southern tip of Africa – good news for surfers, bad news for the remaining teams, because Cape St Francis is also a chokka fishing hotspot and the teams were about to get their first taste of catching squid.

EVERYONE SHOULD KNOW HOW TO MAKE A CAJUN SPICE – IT'S GREAT ON FISH AND CHICKEN, AND IS PACKED WITH GREAT FLAVOUR.

FOR 4 CALAMARI STEAKS, YOU'LL NEED:
1 tablespoon of mustard powder
1 tablespoon of ground cumin
salt and black pepper
1 teaspoon of cayenne pepper
2 teaspoons of paprika
2 teaspoons of dried origanum
1 teaspoon of dried thyme
a pinch of brown sugar

Mix everything together and add a small splash of olive oil to prevent it from sticking when you braai. Rub the Cajun spice on to the calamari steaks, and if your steaks aren't completely covered make another batch of the spice.

Braai the steaks on a grid over medium hot coals for 3 minutes a side – if you overcook the calamari, it will become rubbery. Serve with tartar sauce (below) and a side of bashed herb and potato salad (page 54) or Marthinus's chips (page 83).

SIMPLY MIX TOGETHER:
1 cup of real mayonnaise
2 tablespoons of capers – chopped
4 tablespoons of gherkins – chopped
4 tablespoons of onion – finely chopped
the zest and juice of 1 lemon
a small handful of parsley – chopped
a small handful of chives – chopped

TARTAR SAUCE

THIS IS REALLY EASY TO MAKE AND IS GREAT WITH SEAFOOD.

ULTIMATE BRAAI RECIPE
JUSTIN BONELLO

ONCE COOKED,
Twice Fried
CHIPS

THIS IS MARTHINUS'S RECIPE AND IT TOOK HIM YEARS TO PERFECT – WITH SO MUCH DEDICATION GOING INTO ONE VEGETABLE YOU KNOW IT HAS TO BE GOOD. THE RECIPE IS SHORT AND SWEET (A LITTLE LIKE HIM) AND SUPER SIMPLE TO MAKE. IT'S A GREAT SIDE TO CALAMARI, BURGERS, STEAKS, OR JUST BY ITSELF.

First pick a friend who has been misbehaving and get him or her to peel the potatoes, jailbird style. Once that's done, quarter them and pop them into a pot of boiling water. Let the potato quarters cook until they pretty much start falling apart. Drain and put them on a tray to let them cool off somewhere windy.

Heat up sufficient oil in a pot and when the temperature reaches 140-150°C, add the chips. Don't chuck all the chips into the oil at once, but rather deep fry in batches to keep the temperature consistent. After 10 minutes, remove the chips and place them on parchment paper and let them cool down again. In true restaurant style, you're going to make the chips to order, so at the same time that you're making the calamari steaks and tartar sauce (page 80) get your braai buddy to finish off the chips. Heat up a new pot of oil (to the same temperature as above) and deep fry in batches until golden and crispy (but still soft and fluffy on the inside).

Put the chips on clean parchment paper, drain excess oil and toss with coarse sea salt. Boom! You and your friends are about to eat the best potato chips EVER!

YOU'LL NEED:
- 1 Cadac gas braai
- 1.5 kg potatoes
- vegetable oil
- parchment paper
- salt

POTATO CHIP TIP:
A good potato should take 4 to 5 minutes to become golden brown, crispy on the outside and still soft on the inside.

If the chips become golden after a minute or less, it means you've got a bad batch of potatoes with too high a sugar and water content, and chances are slim that they'll crisp up (not so lekker, but still edible).

Seafood BASKET

YOU'LL NEED:

- 3 oysters per person
- a couple of red chillies – thinly sliced
- a couple of cloves of garlic – crushed and chopped
- a couple of knobs of butter
- the juice of 1 lemon
- fresh rocket leaves

FOR BRAAI'D YELLOWTAIL:

- a couple of knobs of butter
- a couple of cloves of garlic – crushed and chopped
- 1 fresh yellowtail – cleaned and filleted and cut into friend-size portions

FOR DEEP FRIED CALAMARI:

- a couple of tubes of cleaned calamari
- cake flour
- fish spice (dried basil, dill, garlic powder, onion powder, dried oregano and dried lemon zest)
- paprika
- salt and pepper
- vegetable oil

POACHED BUTTER OYSTERS: First up, count your friends. Because this is part of a platter, don't go too big on the oysters (unless you picked loads off the rocks yourself, in which case go crazy and reward yourself). Three oysters per friend should be enough as part of the meal.

Shuck as many fresh oysters as you need by simply sticking a screwdriver into the side of the oyster and wiggling it around until the shell opens up. The trick is to force it open without breaking the shell. If you spot a pearl, don't tell anyone, put it in your pocket and give it to your lady friend when you're in trouble. Loosen the flesh from the shell and keep the oysters (still inside the shells) on ice until you're ready to cook them.

Next, heat a large fireproof pan over medium coals. Melt a big knob of butter and add the chopped garlic, chillies and lemon juice. Drop the oysters out of their shells and into the pan (flesh side down) and lightly poach for about 6 minutes or until the flesh plumps up. Remove the oysters from the heat, pop them back on to the shells, drizzle with some of the butter sauce and serve with fresh rocket and extra lemon wedges.

BRAAI'D YELLOWTAIL: Melt a couple of knobs of butter (probably half a block) in a saucepan and add the garlic. Next, take the yellowtail fillets and place them over medium coals, skin side down. Braai slowly, basting the flesh side every so often with the melted butter and garlic. Once the skin side is crisp, turn the fish over on to the flesh side and braai for a couple of minutes. Remove from the heat, baste one last time and serve.

DEEP FRIED CALAMARI: Cut the cleaned calamari tubes into rings, no thicker than 1 cm wide. Mix together about half a cup of cake flour with a couple of pinches of fish spice, paprika, salt and pepper. Dust the rings in the flour mixture simply by tossing them around inside the bowl.

Heat up a fireproof pot over hot coals. Add a generous glug of oil and when it's hot, carefully place the calamari tubes in it. Deep fry for about 3 minutes or until the cake flour turns golden. Remove from the heat and scoop the calamari on to a paper towel to drain.

 SERVE ONE BASKET PER FRIEND WITH TWICE FRIED CHIPS (PAGE 83) AND TARTAR SAUCE (PAGE 80).

JUST LIKE COOKING ON AN OPEN FIRE RUNS IN OUR VEINS, SO DOES PACKING UP THE CAR (WITH EVERYTHING BUT THE KITCHEN SINK) AND SETTING OFF WITH OUR FRIENDS AND FAMILY TO GO CAMPING. I THINK IT ALL STARTED WITH THE GREAT TREK – THOSE FOLKS HAD SLEEPING UNDER THE STARS DOWN TO A FINE ART. AND ANYWAY, WHO CAN BLAME US FOR OUR LOVE OF PITCHING TENTS IN THE MIDDLE OF NOWHERE? SOUTH AFRICANS JUST HAVE TO TRAVEL TWO HOURS OUT OF THEIR SUBURB TO EXPERIENCE OUR INCREDIBLE OUTDOORS. OUR AMAZING DESTINATIONS PUT OUR CAMPERS IN A WHOLE DIFFERENT LEAGUE FROM THE REST OF THE WORLD. FROM FESTIVALS LIKE AFRIKABURN IN THE KAROO, ROCKING THE DAISIES AND OPPIKOPPI TO COMPLETELY SECLUDED GETAWAYS, VIEWS OF CLIFFS, SLEEPING ON THE BEACH, ILLEGAL CAMPING ON FARMS . . . YOU GET THE IDEA. IN SOUTH AFRICA CAMPING IS NOT JUST A HOLIDAY. IT'S A CULTURE.

IF YOU'RE A CAMPING NOVICE, FIRST OFF, WELCOME TO THE CLUB. THERE'S NO GOING BACK. AND SECOND, HERE ARE SOME BASIC THINGS THAT YOU NEED TO KNOW.

Remember the obvious. Sleeping bag, roll-out mattress, mosquito repellent, hiking shoes, rain jacket, hat, sunscreen, swimsuit, cutlery, cups, plates, at least one decent knife, board games, braai grid, tongs, potjie pot and fishing gear.

Just say yes. If your wife or girlfriend tries to squeeze something into the fully packed car just as you're about to leave, let her. Chances are pretty good that you'll actually need it.

Take a pillow. You can still be an extreme camper even if you're sleeping with your down-feather pillow.

Take some fold-up chairs. Maybe I'm giving my age away here, but I'm past the stage of sitting on sharp rocks, logs or just on my butt. Plus, if you're clever, you'll get a camping chair with a drinks holder. Chances of drink spillage have just been reduced by at least 80 per cent. You're welcome.

Start the day early. It's a no-brainer. You are somewhere magnificent where you get to put your feet up and watch the sunrise. (And if you're really good, you'll have some proper *moerkoffie* and homemade rusks.) Also, if you get up early, you have the whole day to play.

Take a couple of good books, including this one. The best part of camping is that there's no TV and no noise to distract you.

Remember to pack your flip-flops. The only unfortunate thing about camping is that you have to share a shower with fellow campers . . . can you imagine the germs and creepy crawlies that you can't see with the naked eye? Just trust me on this.

Buy plenty of firewood on your way to the campsite to light up your African TV. You'll usually find the best type of wood on your way there.

Avoid nasty surprises. Don't forget to check your tent before you leave home. Count the pegs and make sure the tent is in one piece and still waterproof.

Remember to pack your after-dinner-satisfaction. Think red wine, whisky, a case of Castle Draft or a good ol' bottle of Old Brown Sherry to keep you cosy while you stare into the fire or to keep you sane while *that one friend* plays his guitar (badly).

Take a proper cooler box for your meat and other perishables. Take a separate one to keep your beers cold. They are also great as an extra chair or working surface.

Enjoy the view. Spend at least one night sleeping next to the fire, under the stars.

Cowboy CHOW

BERTUS CALLS THIS MEXICAN EGGS, BUT WHEN I MADE IT I FELT LIKE A COWBOY . . . MUST BE SOMETHING TO DO WITH THE BEANS. THIS IS THE PERFECT PICK-ME-UP BREAKFAST AFTER SITTING AROUND THE CAMP FIRE WITH YOUR FRIENDS UNTIL THE WEE HOURS OF THE MORNING. IT'S HEARTY, PACKED TO THE BRIM WITH BACON AND SAUSAGE AND WILL HELP ANY COWBOY (OR GIRL) GET BACK ON THEIR HORSE.

Heat a skillet or non-stick pan on medium to hot coals, add a splash of olive oil, then fry the sausages, bacon, onion and mushrooms. Add the tomatoes and beans when the meat is almost cooked. As soon as everything is simmering nicely, make eight little hollows in the contents of the pan and crack an egg into each. Sprinkle the chopped chilli and garlic over the top, cover with foil and cook over low coals until the eggs are to your liking.

Grab some toasted bruschetta (page 67), gather your friends around the fire and let them scoop the eggy chow out of the pan with the bread. Best part of this dish? You'll have no plates to wash afterwards, because even the pan should be licked clean.

YOU'LL NEED:

- a splash of olive oil
- 8 free range pork sausages – kept whole
- 1 packet of free range streaky bacon – chopped
- 1 onion, chopped finely
- 1 packet of mushrooms – use your favourite kind
- 2 handfuls of cherry tomatoes
- 1 tin of good ol' baked beans
- 8 free range eggs
- 3 chillies – chopped, seeds removed
- 2 cloves of garlic – finely chopped

★ **THIS WILL FEED ABOUT 4 TO 6 FRIENDS.**

Tubby's FRENCH TOAST

THIS IS A GREAT TWIST ON TRADITIONAL FRENCH TOAST. FIRST FIGURE OUT HOW HUNGRY YOUR FRIENDS ARE – ONE OR TWO SLICES OF BREAD PER PERSON SHOULD DO THE TRICK.

Get your braai buddy to heat up two medium-sized skillets over hot coals and fry the bacon in one pan and the banana the other. While he's busy with that, you do the French toast. It sounds tricky, but it's not.

Cut a circle out of the centre of each slice of bread. Give the discs of bread to your braai buddy to fry in the same pan as the bacon until crispy (think crouton).

Whisk two eggs, a dash of milk and salt and pepper. Heat up a large skillet over hot coals and add a knob of butter. Soak the bread in the egg mixture and once the butter has melted, gently place the slices of eggy bread in the pan. As soon as the bottom part has browned, flip it over and break an egg into the hole in the centre of the toast. Do this with each piece of toast in the pan. Cook until the other side of the toast has browned, then flip it over one last time just to cook the egg white in the holes. The trick is not to overcook the egg, but rather to have the yolk perfectly soft and the white firm. Remove from the pan, and place on a plate with the egg sunny side up.

Top with a slice of your favourite cheese to melt, a couple of rashers of bacon, a couple of slices of banana and a crouton on top. (You're going to dip the crouton into the perfectly soft egg yolk, like nursery soft-boiled eggs and toast soldiers.) *Voila!* French toast just got a (w)hole lot tastier!

WHO DARES, WINS ★ FRIENDS

★

YOU'LL NEED:

- a couple of rashers of streaky bacon
- a couple of bananas – sliced
- a couple of thick (about 1 cm) slices of white bread (you can use brown)
- 2 eggs, a dash of milk, salt and pepper
- slices of your favourite cheese
- as many extra eggs as slices of French toast

PS: If all of this is a little too French for you, or you find yourself strapped for time, rather make my eggy pimped braai broodjies on page 94. Just as delicious and a lot less work.

Pimp My BRAAI Broodjie

BRAAI BROODJIES ARE USUALLY THE TOMATO AND ONION KIND THAT GET DEVOURED BEFORE THE REST OF THE BRAAI IS READY. BUT HAVE YOU EVER THOUGHT ABOUT MAKING A BRAAI BROODJIE THE MAIN ATTRACTION? LET'S FACE IT – THERE ARE FEW THINGS IN LIFE THAT CAN BEAT THE TASTE OF A GREAT SANDWICH.

ULTIMATE BRAAI RECIPE
JUSTIN BONELLO

★ FRENCH TOAST SARMIES

A QUICK BREAKFAST FOR 4 FRIENDS

- about 14 rashers of bacon
- 6-8 eggs
- a splash of milk
- salt and pepper
- 3 large bananas
- 8 slices of white bread
- golden syrup (optional)

Chop the bacon roughly and fry in a skillet over hot coals until crisp. Drain on kitchen paper. Whisk the eggs with a splash of milk in a deep flat bowl and season with a pinch of salt and cracked black pepper. Peel and slice the bananas and place them on top of 4 slices of bread. Top with the bacon and, if you have a sweet tooth, drizzle with golden syrup. Make 4 sandwiches with the remaining slices of bread, and then submerge the whole sandwich in the egg mixture to soak both sides. Immediately put the sandwiches on a sandwich grill and toast over medium coals on both sides until golden, crispy and cooked through.

★ LAMB PITA

IF YOU DON'T LIKE LEFTOVER LAMB, THEN YOU CAN NEVER BE MY FRIEND. IF YOU DO, HERE'S A GREAT WAY TO MAKE AN AWESOME LUNCH.

- 2-3 handfuls of leftover lamb – shredded
- a couple of rounds of feta – crumbled
- olive oil
- 4 pita breads
- about a cup of Greek yoghurt
- about a cup of cucumber – chopped
- a couple of cloves of garlic – crushed and chopped
- a handful of dill – chopped
- a small handful of mint – chopped
- a generous squeeze of lemon juice
- salt and cracked black pepper

Toss the shredded lamb, feta, pepper and a little olive oil together, then spoon this mixture into pita breads. Place in a sandwich grill and toast until the lamb has heated through and the bread is golden. Mix the yoghurt, cucumber, garlic, dill, mint, lemon juice and seasoning together and spoon into the toasted lamb pitas.

★ MAFIA MEATBALL SUBS

A HEARTY LUNCH FOR FOUR PEOPLE. SERVE WITH POTATO SALAD (PAGE 54) OR BY ITSELF.

- 1 onion – chopped
- a couple of pinches of fresh oregano – chopped
- about 1 tablespoon of ground cumin
- a couple of cloves of garlic – crushed and finely chopped
- a couple of chillies – deseeded and finely chopped
- salt and pepper
- about 500 g beef mince
- a big handful of breadcrumbs
- olive oil
- 4 paninis or 1 large baguette
- tomato chutney (see page 182)
- Parmesan shavings

Mix the onion, oregano, cumin, garlic, chilli, salt, pepper, mince and breadcrumbs together. Roll the meatball mixture into balls, then fry over hot coals in an oiled skillet until cooked through (but still pink on the inside). Slice the paninis open and hollow out a little of the soft bread centre to create space for the meatballs. Drizzle with olive oil, season with salt and pepper and then place the meatballs in the hollows. Scoop tomato chutney over the meatballs, sprinkle with Parmesan shavings and close up the roll. Place in a sandwich grid over medium to cool coals and grill until the cheese has melted and the paninis have turned golden and crispy.

Camping Salads

Trying to keep fresh ingredients crisp and delicious is almost impossible on a camping trip, unless you have a fancy car that comes with a built-in fridge – but most of us don't. Chances are that you'll have some odds and ends tucked away in your trusty cooler bag that you can toss together to create interesting and tasty salads. Some of these ingredients are not my normal style, but they are things that you can whip together in the great outdoors. On another note, some of the salads call for fresh herbs, but if you don't have any, use dried instead. It's not as effective, but will do the job just fine when you're camping.

There really are no rules in this space, but if you prefer to plan ahead, here are three *lekker* and super simple salads you can *gooi* together – ideal for that old-school camping holiday. These salads will also keep in your cooler box for more than a day, so pack some empty ice cream containers for easy storing of leftovers.

Pearled Wheat Salad

Boil a 500 g packet of pearled wheat in chicken stock for about an hour. Drain it and mix with 1 chopped red pepper, 4 sliced leeks, about 1 cup of chopped dried peaches, half a packet of sultanas, 1 cup of mayonnaise, 100 ml chutney, 10 ml curry powder, and salt and black pepper. This salad is really good if you let it stand overnight to allow the flavours to develop.

Wild Rice Salad

Cook a cup of wild and brown rice (combined), drain and let it cool. Then mix in finely chopped red onion and red pepper, 2 sticks of chopped celery, a handful of both chopped mint and coriander, a cup of dried cranberries and ½ a cup of macadamia nuts. Drizzle over a dressing of ¼ cup of olive oil, 3 tablespoons of basil pesto, 3 teaspoons of mint jelly, and salt and cracked black pepper.

Chickpea Salad

Mix together 1 tin of drained chickpeas, 1 finely chopped red onion, 1 chopped red pepper and 4 sticks of chopped celery, half a tin of peas, about 2 raw mealies (cut off the cob) and two handfuls of torn basil leaves. Toss the salad in a dressing of fresh ginger (1 big chunk, minced), a clove of crushed garlic (finely chopped), 2 kaffir lime leaves (shredded), 1 chopped chilli, a pinch of brown sugar, the zest of 1 lime, a generous splash of olive oil, 2 tablespoons of fish sauce, about 1 tablespoon of sweet chilli sauce, a handful of chopped mint and the juice of about half a lime.

ULTIMATE BRAAI RECIPE
JUSTIN BONELLO

Braai Spuds

Stab one end of each potato with an apple corer (lengthwise) and force it through to the centre of the potato (just like you would when coring an apple). Keep the core of potato.

WE ALL KNOW HOW TO BAKE A POTATO ON THE FIRE. SO WHY NOT ADD SOME FLAVOUR? THIS IS A SIMPLE WAY TO TRANSFORM THE OLD-SCHOOL BRAAI'D POTATO INTO SOMETHING REALLY SPECIAL.

Now you're ready to stuff the potatoes with whatever you like. For instance, using a teaspoon scoop a flavoured butter into the potato tunnel until it's completely filled up. Use the potato core to plug the end of each stuffed tunnel so that the stuffing stays inside. Now wrap each potato in foil and place alongside the same coals you're going to be cooking your meat on. Turn the spuds every now and then to ensure they cook evenly and to prevent them from burning. Remove the potatoes from the heat after about 50 minutes and check if they're cooked. If they still feel hard, pop them back on to the coals for a while.

HERE ARE A FEW OF MY FAVOURITE STUFFINGS, BUT YOU SHOULD EXPERIMENT TO SEE WHAT YOU LIKE BEST. EACH RECIPE PROVIDES ENOUGH STUFFING FOR ABOUT 4 TO 5 LARGE POTATOES. SO COUNT YOUR FRIENDS AND DO THE MATHS.

★ HERBY OLIVE AND SUNDRIED TOMATO
BASH ALL THE INGREDIENTS TOGETHER.

- a couple of knobs of softened butter
- a handful of parsley – chopped
- a small handful of sundried tomato – chopped finely
- a couple of sprigs of thyme – leaves removed from the stalks
- a handful of calamata olives – pips removed and chopped
- a couple of cloves of garlic – crushed and chopped
- 2-3 anchovies – chopped
- zest of 1 lemon

★ HARISSA AND HERB
MASH ALL THE INGREDIENTS TOGETHER.

- a couple of knobs of butter
- zest of 1 lemon, or a couple of preserved lemon rinds – chopped
- a couple of cloves of garlic – crushed
- a handful of fresh coriander – chopped
- a couple of spoonfuls of Harissa paste

★ CHEESY ONION AND CHILLI
MIX ALL THE INGREDIENTS TOGETHER.

- 1 bunch of spring onions – finely chopped
- ½ red onion – chopped
- a large handful of grated mature cheddar
- a large handful of grated Parmesan
- a handful of parsley – chopped
- a handful of fresh coriander – chopped
- a couple of chillies – seeds removed and finely chopped
- a couple of cloves of garlic – crushed and chopped
- a couple of knobs of softened butter

★ CAPER BUTTER
MIX ALL THE INGREDIENTS TOGETHER.

- a few knobs of softened butter
- a couple of cloves of garlic – crushed
- a sprig of rosemary – chopped
- a handful of fresh basil – chopped
- a handful of grated Parmesan
- ½ onion – finely chopped
- a couple of spoonfuls of capers – chopped

Stuffed
ONIONS

THIS IS AN EASY WAY TO TAKE THE HUMBLE ONION TO A WHOLE NEW CULINARY LEVEL. IT IS ALSO THE PERFECT CAMPING SIDE-DISH RECIPE BECAUSE IT USES BASIC INGREDIENTS THAT WON'T SPOIL EASILY.

YOU'LL NEED:
a couple of rashers of streaky bacon
about a cup of cream cheese
a bunch of spring onions – chopped
a handful of fresh coriander – chopped
salt and pepper
a couple of chillies – seeds removed and finely chopped
a couple of cloves of garlic – crushed and finely chopped
5 whole onions (skins and all)

Chop up the bacon and fry over hot coals until crispy. Set aside to cool slightly on kitchen paper. Mix the cream cheese with the spring onions, coriander, salt, pepper, chilli and garlic. Add the bacon and stir it in.

Next, take the onions and slice a cross in each from sprout side to root side making sure you leave a couple of centimetres uncut at the root side (the onion needs to be kept whole). Carefully open the top of the wedges and stuff with the cream cheese mixture. Place the onions, stalk side down (that's the side that hasn't been cut through) on top of a sheet of foil and pull up the sides to form a parcel. Make sure there are no holes in your parcels. Put the onions next to (not on top of) medium to hot coals for about 40 to 45 minutes. Turn them often to ensure they cook evenly. When the parcel feels soft, you're ready to serve.

Engine Stew
MYTH BUSTER!

IF YOU EVER PLAN ONE OF THOSE ROAD TRIPS WHERE YOU KNOW YOU'RE GOING TO ARRIVE AFTER DARK (WHICH IS ALWAYS THE CASE WITH ME AND MY CREW), THEN ENGINE STEW IS THE PERFECT DINNERTIME SOLUTION. SIMPLY PREPARE THE STEW YOU WOULD LIKE FOR DINNER BEFORE YOU LEAVE HOME. PUT IT ON THE MANIFOLD (THAT'S A PART OF YOUR CAR'S ENGINE) ABOUT 500 KILOMETRES FROM YOUR DESTINATION AND TUCK IN AS SOON AS YOU'VE UNPACKED THE BOOT (AND THE ENGINE). THIS IS GAL POWER'S RECIPE.

First sauté the onions and pepper until soft. Add the paprika, cumin, coriander and finely chopped chillies, and then add then the beef cubes. Stir until all the meat is covered in the spices. Add the chopped tomatoes and stir continuously for about 2 minutes, then add the red wine (none for yourself though – you're driving!), the diced carrots, leeks and potatoes and enough beef stock to cover the contents. Lastly, add the herbs and season with salt and pepper to taste.

Now for the fun part. Get your hands on a tin foil roasting pan. Go to your car and open the bonnet. Look for a level place where the heat of the engine will radiate through the roasting tin – I used the manifold. (Heat transference is very important, otherwise you will have no stew.) Shape the roasting pan so that it will fit firmly, but beware of the fan belt and any other moving parts. Go back into the kitchen, fill the roasting tin with the prepared stew and seal the whole lot in a couple of layers of foil. Go back to your car and place the stew on top of the manifold. Secure it with some soft wire so that it won't fall over. Check your oil and water, close the bonnet and drive. (Don't tell your insurance company what you're about to get up to.)

About 500 kilometres later the stew should be cooked perfectly, and the beef will be tender.

YOU'LL NEED:

- 1 car that can travel 500 km (or 6 hours)
- a couple of onions – chopped
- 1 green pepper – chopped
- a couple of pinches of paprika, cumin and ground coriander
- a couple of chillies – seeds removed and finely chopped
- fatty beef shin – cut into cubes
- a couple of tomatoes – chopped
- a couple of glugs of red wine
- a handful of carrots – chopped
- a couple of leeks – washed and sliced
- about 3 potatoes – peeled and cubed
- about ½ cup of beef stock
- chopped thyme, rosemary and sage
- salt and pepper to taste
- 1 x foil roasting tin

WILD COAST
U B
M
TRANSKEI

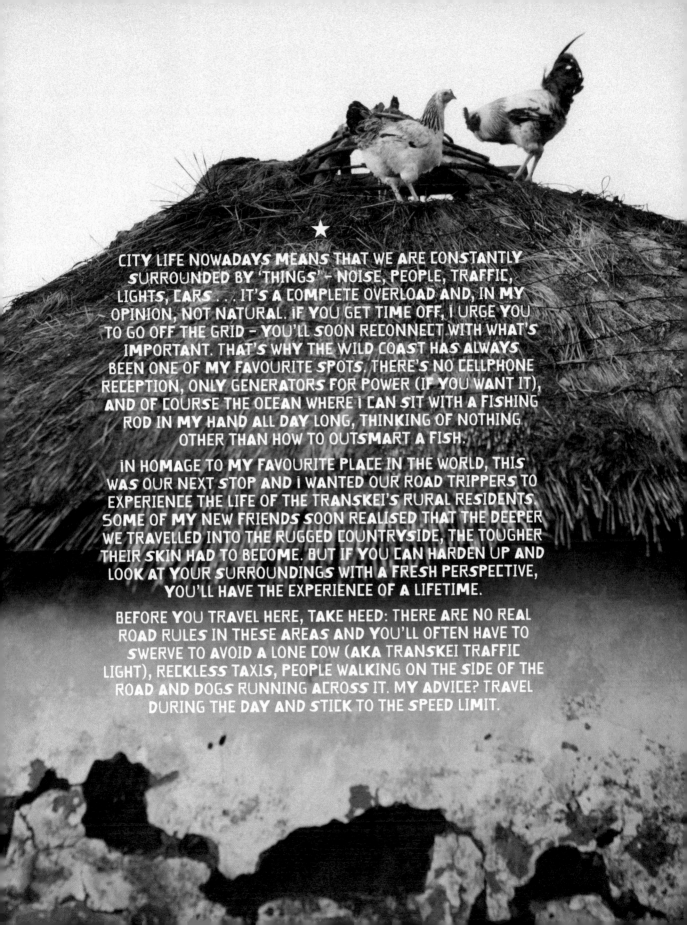

★

CITY LIFE NOWADAYS MEANS THAT WE ARE CONSTANTLY SURROUNDED BY 'THINGS' – NOISE, PEOPLE, TRAFFIC, LIGHTS, CARS . . . IT'S A COMPLETE OVERLOAD AND, IN MY OPINION, NOT NATURAL. IF YOU GET TIME OFF, I URGE YOU TO GO OFF THE GRID – YOU'LL SOON RECONNECT WITH WHAT'S IMPORTANT. THAT'S WHY THE WILD COAST HAS ALWAYS BEEN ONE OF MY FAVOURITE SPOTS. THERE'S NO CELLPHONE RECEPTION, ONLY GENERATORS FOR POWER (IF YOU WANT IT), AND OF COURSE THE OCEAN WHERE I CAN SIT WITH A FISHING ROD IN MY HAND ALL DAY LONG, THINKING OF NOTHING OTHER THAN HOW TO OUTSMART A FISH.

IN HOMAGE TO MY FAVOURITE PLACE IN THE WORLD, THIS WAS OUR NEXT STOP AND I WANTED OUR ROAD TRIPPERS TO EXPERIENCE THE LIFE OF THE TRANSKEI'S RURAL RESIDENTS. SOME OF MY NEW FRIENDS SOON REALISED THAT THE DEEPER WE TRAVELLED INTO THE RUGGED COUNTRYSIDE, THE TOUGHER THEIR SKIN HAD TO BECOME. BUT IF YOU CAN HARDEN UP AND LOOK AT YOUR SURROUNDINGS WITH A FRESH PERSPECTIVE, YOU'LL HAVE THE EXPERIENCE OF A LIFETIME.

BEFORE YOU TRAVEL HERE, TAKE HEED: THERE ARE NO REAL ROAD RULES IN THESE AREAS AND YOU'LL OFTEN HAVE TO SWERVE TO AVOID A LONE COW (AKA TRANSKEI TRAFFIC LIGHT), RECKLESS TAXIS, PEOPLE WALKING ON THE SIDE OF THE ROAD AND DOGS RUNNING ACROSS IT. MY ADVICE? TRAVEL DURING THE DAY AND STICK TO THE SPEED LIMIT.

Village FEAST

ALL THESE RECIPES COMBINED WILL FEED A SMALL VILLAGE SO ADJUST THE QUANTITIES TO YOUR REQUIREMENTS . . . UNLESS YOU'RE ACTUALLY PLANNING ON FEEDING A SMALL VILLAGE.

SAMP AND BEANS ★

Place the samp, beans and a generous pinch of salt in a big potjie then pour in water until the samp and bean mix is just covered. Place the pot over hot coals and bring to the boil. Scrape out some coals to reduce the heat slightly, cover the pot and let the samp and beans simmer for about an hour or until soft. At the same time, add water to another potjie and when it starts boiling add the potato cubes. Boil until the potatoes are soft then remove from the heat and drain. Using a potato masher, mash the potatoes until smooth. Add a bit of salt, but don't overdo it.

When the samp and beans are cooked, remove from the heat and rinse thoroughly in cold water. Drain and set aside. Next, take a large skillet, add a big knob of butter and the chopped onions. Fry until the onions are soft, then add about a tablespoon of curry powder, the chopped tomatoes, vegetable stock, fresh thyme and salt and pepper to taste. Add the samp, beans and mashed potatoes and mix thoroughly. Simmer uncovered for about 5 minutes, remove it from the heat and finish it off by stirring in a couple of knobs of butter.

GAL POWER

YOU'LL NEED:
- samp and bean mix (soaked)
- about 5 potatoes – peeled and chopped into cubes
- a knob of butter
- 2 onions – chopped
- 1 tablespoon of curry powder
- 4 tomatoes – chopped
- ½ litre of vegetable stock
- a small handful of fresh thyme – chopped
- salt and pepper to taste

GRILLED CHICKEN
GAL POWER
YOU'LL NEED:

- 2 whole chickens – spatchcocked
- olive oil
- coarse salt and black pepper
- a small handful of fresh thyme – chopped

Place the chickens in a pot and cover with cold water. Turn the heat up and simmer until just cooked. Take the chickens out of the water, drain and cool, then brush with olive oil, and sprinkle with fresh thyme and salt and pepper to taste. Place them in a sandwich grid and braai over medium hot coals until the skin is crispy.

MOROGO
WHO DARES, WINS
YOU'LL NEED:

- a big knob of butter
- 1 smallish onion – thinly sliced
- 2 cloves of garlic – crushed and chopped
- 2 bunches of fresh spinach – washed and chopped
- 1 parboiled potato – skin removed and finely diced
- salt and pepper to taste

First up, melt the butter and fry the onion. Spinach loves butter, so use as much as you want to. Add the chopped garlic and fry until brown. Add the spinach in handfuls, then pop the lid on to create some liquid. (Do not add any water!) When the spinach has wilted, remove the lid to let some of the juice evaporate. Add the potato, more butter, salt and a couple of cracks of black pepper. Stir and serve.

CHICKEN CURRY À LA PONDO
WHO DARES, WINS
YOU'LL NEED:

- canola oil
- 1 teaspoon whole jeera (whole cumin seeds)
- 3-4 cloves of garlic – chopped
- 1 large chunk of ginger – chopped
- 1 onion – sliced
- a couple of teaspoons of mild curry powder (as much or as little as you can handle)
- 2 whole free range chickens – cut into pieces
- cold water
- a knob of butter

Pour some canola oil into a large potjie, add the whole jeera and watch the seeds burst open and release their flavour (but don't stick your head too deep into the potjie). Add the chopped garlic, ginger and onion, mix with the jeera and fry until golden. Next add a couple of teaspoons of curry powder and stir in well. Keep tossing it around – it helps the flavour of the curry develop and infuse the onions and oil. Add the chicken pieces and mix thoroughly until they are all covered with the masala mixture. Add a couple of cups of cold water and slowly bring to the boil, then scrape some coals away to reduce the temperature. Cover and let the chicken simmer for about an hour or until cooked through. Before you serve it, scoop off any excess oil floating on top, then stir in a knob of butter.

CHAKALAKA
GAL POWER

There are a million different versions of this – this one is Gal Power's and it's a definite winner!

YOU'LL NEED:

- canola oil
- 2-3 onions – chopped
- 1 green, 1 yellow and 1 red pepper – chopped
- a couple of chillies – seeds removed and chopped
- a couple of pinches of chilli powder (depending on how spicy you would like it)
- about 3 carrots – grated
- ½ cabbage, finely chopped
- ½ cup of vegetable stock
- salt and pepper
- a tin of baked beans
- fresh parsley – finely chopped

First, heat up a saucepan and pour in a generous glug of canola oil. When it's hot add the chopped onions, peppers, chillies, chilli powder, grated carrots and cabbage. When the vegetables are cooked, but still crunchy, pour in the vegetable stock, salt and pepper to taste, and add the baked beans and fresh parsley. Let it simmer for a couple of minutes before removing from the heat.

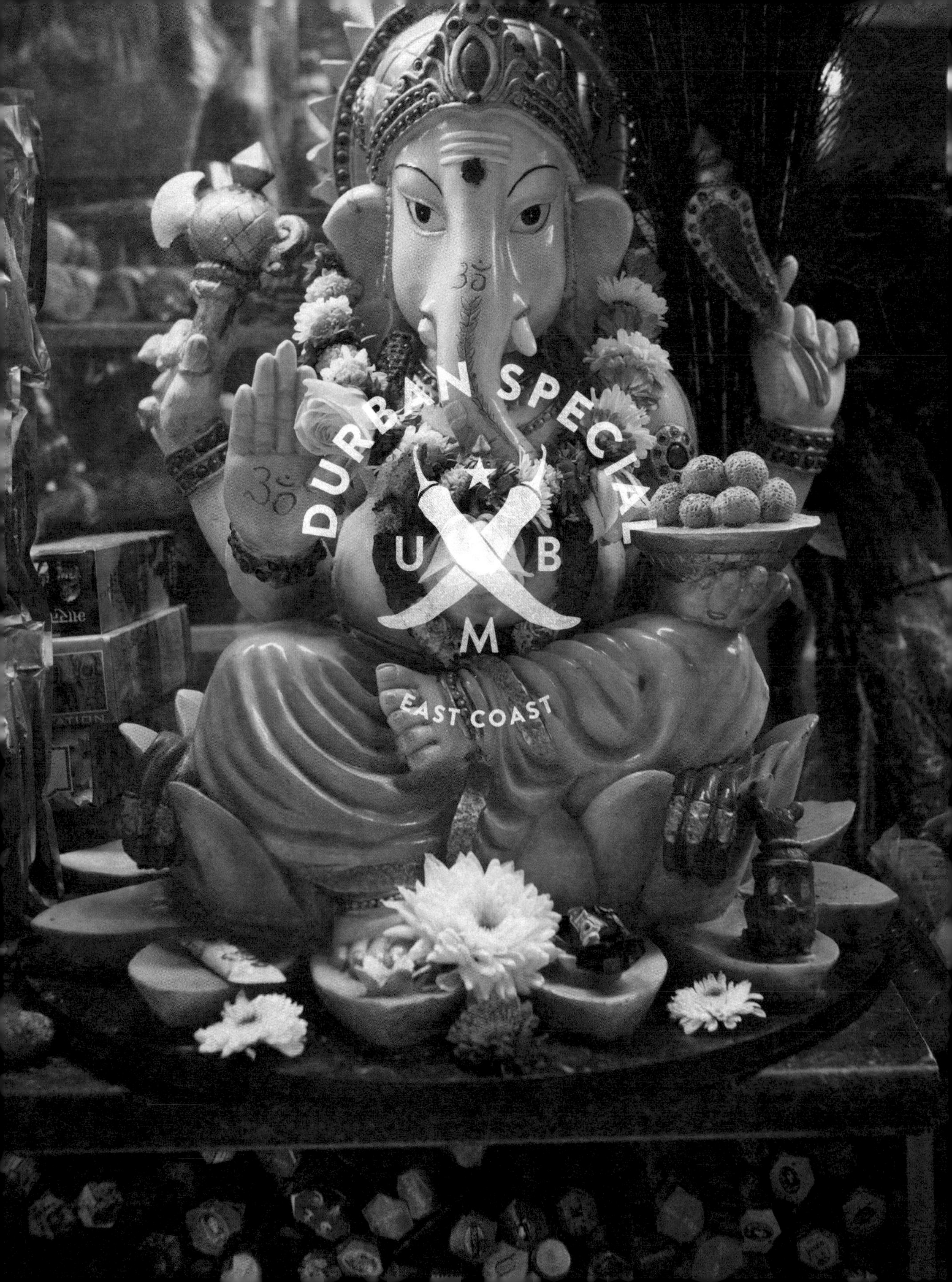
DURBAN SPECIAL
U B
M
EAST COAST

TUMERIC (BORIE) POWDER

AFTER EXPLORING VILLAGE LIFE IN THE HEART OF THE WILD COAST, IT WAS TIME TO PACK UP AND GET THE SHOW BACK ON THE ROAD. WHENEVER I GET OUT INTO THE GREAT OUTDOORS, I'M ALWAYS A BIT BEWILDERED WHEN I GET BACK INTO OUR URBAN JUNGLES, AND I THINK THE ROAD TRIPPERS FELT THE SAME WHEN WE ENTERED THE HUSTLE AND BUSTLE OF KWAZULU-NATAL'S LARGEST CITY.

BUT WE DIDN'T GO THERE FOR THE INFAMOUS COSMOPOLITAN NIGHTLIFE OR TO SURF IN DURBAN'S WARM OCEAN. WE WERE THERE TO SPICE THINGS UP, BECAUSE IN CULINARY TERMS, DURBAN IS SOUTH AFRICA'S LITTLE INDIA AND IS FAMOUS FOR SOME OF THE BEST CURRY JOINTS IN THE COUNTRY.

Extra SPECIAL HERBS Spices

THE SECRET TO A PERFECT, AUTHENTIC INDIAN CURRY IS UNDERSTANDING
WHICH SPICES TO COMBINE, SO MY SUGGESTION IS THAT YOU GET YOUR HANDS
ON A COFFEE GRINDER AND START EXPERIMENTING. IT WON'T BE TOO LONG
BEFORE YOU HAVE YOUR VERY OWN SECRET GARAM MASALA. THE ONLY REALLY
IMPORTANT TIP I CAN GIVE YOU IS THAT THE SPICES HAVE TO BE COOKED FOR AT
LEAST 10 MINUTES. WHEN YOU COOK THE SPICES THE FLAVOURS AND AROMAS
ARE RELEASED AND THE RAW TASTE IS REMOVED. BUT FIRST, YOU NEED TO
UNDERSTAND HOW EACH SPICE WILL ENHANCE YOUR CURRY.

★ JEERA

Jeera seeds (more commonly known as cumin seeds) are very aromatic and are one of the most important spices because they are used in almost every curry dish. Either fry the seeds in hot oil or dry toast them.

★ TURMERIC

Is part of all curry powders and used mostly for its bright yellow colour, although it does impart an earthy flavour.

★ STAR ANISE

This spice is a lot like anise, but more intense in flavour. It is warm, sweet and very aromatic. Very popular in biriyani.

★ CORIANDER SEEDS

This warm, nutty, spicy seed must be dry roasted and is an essential part of any curry powder.

★ CARDOMOM

Often called 'the third most expensive spice', cardamom brings a sweet and aromatic flavour to curries.

★ CINNAMON BARK

Everyone knows cinnamon with its strong aromatic, sweet and warm flavours. Fry in hot oil until the bark unrolls to release its full potential.

★ CHILLI

To the novice, chilli might seem hot, pungent and offensive to the taste buds, but once you're broken in you'll start noticing the sweet, smoky and fruity flavours. You can either use it fresh (for more bite), dried or as a powder.

★ CURRY LEAVES

Bring a fresh and pleasant taste to any curry and are essential for the authentic flavours of Indian curries. Use fresh or dried.

★ WHOLE NUTMEG

Resinous and warm in taste, nutmeg can easily lose its flavour if you use the powder, so try to avoid that. Rather grate from a whole nut just before you add it to the curry.

★ METHI SEEDS

Enhances the flavour of curry and reduces the bitterness of the spice. This is one of the healthiest Indian spices and is popular for its property of lowering blood cholesterol levels.

★ MUSTARD SEEDS

These are either black or dark brown in colour and have a faint curry smell when raw. Fry them in hot oil to release the flavours. They're an excellent complement to fish curries when combined with curry leaves and chillies.

★ GARAM MASALA

Every household has their own secret recipe, and it's usually a combination of jeera, coriander seeds, cardamom seeds, black peppercorns, cinnamon, whole cloves, grated nutmeg, bay leaves and star anise.

Crab Claw

★ CURRY ★

ULTIMATE BRAAI RECIPE — JUSTIN BONELLO

THE FIRST LESSON YOU SHOULD LEARN WHEN YOU GET TO DURBAN IS HOW TO MAKE A PROPER CURRY. THE SECOND? PROBABLY HOW TO SURF. THE LAST LESSON IS HOW TO SPEAK THE UNIQUE DURBAN LINGO – A LANGUAGE THAT ONLY PURE DURBANITES UNDERSTAND. ONCE YOU GET THOSE THINGS RIGHT, LIFE IN DURBS WILL BE (LAAIK) A BREEZE (BRU).

YOU'LL NEED:
- 1 tablespoon of whole mustard seeds
- 1 teaspoon of methi
- 4 large cloves of garlic
- 1 heaped tablespoon of chilli powder (if you like hot curry add an extra tablespoon)
- 2 teaspoons of turmeric
- 1 teaspoon of ground coriander
- 2 teaspoons of ground cumin
- 1 tablespoon of garam masala
- salt and black pepper
- the juice of 1 lemon
- a generous glug of vegetable oil
- 1 onion – finely chopped
- 1 chilli – finely chopped (again, if you like it hot, add an extra chilli)
- 6 tomatoes – chopped
- 1 teaspoon of sugar
- 1 kg crab claws, cleaned
- a generous glug of water
- 6-8 curry leaves

This is my recipe for a spicy crab claw curry taught to me by a sweet Indian lady I met at the Spice Emporium. My advice is to make the first part of the curry the night before to give the flavours time to infuse and then finish it on the braai the next day.

I'm not usually the kind of guy who sticks to exact quantities, but I've learned that when it comes to boerewors, baking and curries, it's important to stick to the rules to avoid any nasty surprises later.

In a mortar and pestle, bash the mustard seeds, methi and garlic until finely ground. Mix this with the chilli powder, turmeric, coriander, cumin, garam masala, a pinch of salt and pepper and the lemon juice.

Next, go wash your hands . . . trust me. Now, heat the oil in a large skillet over medium coals. Add the onion, fresh chilli, masala (that's the spice mixture you just made) tomatoes and sugar and braise until softened. Stick the tip of your finger in and taste the curry paste to check if you might need a bit more salt. Lightly bash the crab claws with whatever heavy object you have close to you – this will loosen the meat and allow more flavour to go into the crab when cooking. Add the crab claws, water and curry leaves to the curry paste, toss around and simmer for about 8 minutes. Now you can either braai the crab immediately or you can pop it in the fridge to marinate overnight and let the flavours develop and infuse.

Place the claws on a grid over medium coals, and put the remaining curry sauce in a potjie to simmer. Because the crab is already par-cooked, you don't want to braai it for too long – just until the shells are slightly charred on both sides. Put it back into the fragrant curry sauce and serve with lemon wedges and rice or fresh bread (and ice cold beer to soothe your burning lips). *Lekker!*

Sugar Cane
★ KEBABS ★

THE GREAT THING ABOUT BRAAIING WITH SUGAR CANE IS THAT IT ADDS A NATURAL SWEETNESS TO THE MEAT THAT'S SKEWERED ON TO IT. THE OTHER BONUS IS THAT YOU GET TO CHEW ON THE KEBAB STICKS AFTER YOU'VE EATEN OFF ALL THE MEAT, SO NO DESSERT NEEDED AND NOTHING GOES TO WASTE. IF YOU EVER FIND YOURSELF IN KWAZULU-NATAL, GET YOUR HANDS ON SUGAR CANE (READILY AVAILABLE NEXT TO THE ROAD OR, IF YOU'RE A LITTLE BORING, AT MOST SHOPS) AND BRAAI SOME THAI-INSPIRED PORK FILLET SUGAR CANE KEBABS.

Remove the outer layer of the lemon grass and finely chop up the inside. Take a mortar and pestle and add to it the chopped lemon grass, lime zest, chilli, ginger, garlic, basil and coriander. Grind and bash everything until the flavours are released then add the fish sauce, soya sauce and lime juice. Next, cut the pork fillet into cubes and pour the marinade over the meat. Let it rest in the marinade for about an hour.

Peel off the hard outer layer of the sugar cane and cut it into makeshift kebab skewers. Don't worry if the points of the skewers aren't sharp – pork fillet is so soft that the sugar cane will easily pierce through the meat. Put about 4 cubes of pork on to each kebab until all the meat has been used up. Braai over medium hot coals until cooked through (no longer than 20 minutes) – but it can be served pink on the inside.

YOU'LL NEED:
- 1 stalk of lemon grass
- the zest and juice of 2 limes
- about 2 chillies – finely chopped
- a big chunk of ginger – grated
- 3 cloves of garlic – crushed and chopped
- a handful of basil – chopped
- a handful of fresh coriander – chopped
- a splash of fish sauce
- a decent splash of Kikkoman soya sauce
- 1 medium-sized pork fillet
- 1 stick of sugar cane

**SERVE AS PART OF AN OOPSIE PLATTER (PAGE 138)
WITH A BUCKET OF ICE COLD CIDER.**

Gourmet
BOERIE TOPPINGS

SOMETIMES A DELICIOUS TOPPING CAN SAVE THE WORST BOEREWORS. AND SOMETIMES IT MAKES THE BEST BOEREWORS ROLLS TASTE EVEN BETTER. GO TO YOUR LOCAL BUTCHERY AND GET YOUR HANDS ON THE TRUSTY BOEREWORS YOU ALWAYS BUY. MAKE YOUR FAVOURITE TOPPING, BUY SOME FRESH ROLLS AND PACK IT ALL INTO YOUR TRUSTY COOLER BAG. GOOI IT ALL ON THE BACK OF YOUR BAKKIE (REMEMBER TO PUT UP YOUR STORMERS FLAGS . . . ESPECIALLY IF YOU FIND YOURSELF IN SHARK TERRITORY) AND GO PARK OUTSIDE THE STADIUM. LIGHT YOUR FIRES, PUT OUT THE CAMPING CHAIRS FOR THE LADIES, POUR THE DRINKS AND GET THE PRE-RUGBY MATCH *GEES* STARTED!

CHILLIDOG ★

Heat the oil and then fry the chopped onion, bacon bits, thyme, cumin and chilli powder until soft and fragrant. Add the crushed garlic, tomato paste and beef mince and fry until the mince is almost cooked. Next, add the canned tomatoes, cocktail tomatoes, stock, vinegar and seasoning and simmer uncovered for about 30 minutes until the sauce has reduced.

Serve spooned on to boerewors rolls with a dollop of sour cream and grated mozzarella.

ULTIMATE BRAAI RECIPE
JUSTIN BONELLO

YOU'LL NEED:
- olive oil
- 1 onion – finely chopped
- ½ packet of bacon – finely chopped
- a couple of sprigs of thyme – finely chopped
- a couple of pinches of ground cumin
- a couple of pinches of chilli powder (add extra if you like it hot)
- 2-3 cloves of garlic – crushed and finely chopped
- 2 teaspoons of tomato paste
- about 400 g lean beef mince
- 1 can of chopped tomatoes (the proper Italian kind)
- a handful of cocktail tomatoes
- a cup of beef stock
- a generous glug of red wine vinegar
- salt and pepper

★ THE PATAT

He's a top-notch chef so, trust me, this topping is a winner. This recipe has nothing to do with Sweet Potato, but rather with Bertus's dog (according to Bertus, his best friend in the whole wide world). Because we were on the road for 52 days and Bertus was Patat-less (and feeling very sad), I promised him I would mention Patat in the book, so here we go . . .

Mix all the ingredients together and spoon on to boerewors rolls.

YOU'LL NEED:
- 1 cup of red cabbage – finely chopped
- 1 cup of green cabbage – finely chopped
- a couple of spoonfuls of chopped dill
- a couple of spoonfuls of real mayonnaise
- a generous dollop (or two) of wholegrain mustard
- a squeeze of lemon
- black pepper

CARAMELISED ONIONS ★

Heat the oil and butter in a skillet over medium coals. Add the onions and rosemary and leave to soften, then add a splash of red wine vinegar, sugar and mustard and cook it over a low heat until caramelised. Serve spooned on boerewors rolls.

YOU'LL NEED:
- olive oil
- a big knob of butter
- about 6 red onions – finely sliced
- a couple of sprigs of rosemary – finely chopped
- a splash of red wine vinegar
- a tablespoon of brown sugar
- a couple of dollops of wholegrain mustard

CRANBERRY, WATERCRESS AND DEEP-FRIED CAMEMBERT

YOU'LL NEED:
1 round Camembert
cake flour
1 egg – beaten
breadcrumbs
a few spoonfuls of cranberry sauce
juice of ½ lemon
black pepper
a couple of handfuls of watercress

The trick to this topping is to serve it while the cheese is still hot so that when you bite into it, it will melt all over the boerewors.

Cut the Camembert round into 8 wedges. Toss in the flour, dunk in the egg, coat with breadcrumbs and deep-fry until golden. Mix the cranberry sauce with lemon and black pepper, spoon over boerewors rolls and top with watercress and deep-fried Camembert.

ULTIMATE BRAAI RECIPE
JUSTIN BONELLO

★

WELL KNOWN FOR ITS STUD, BEEF AND DAIRY
FARMS AND SOME OF THE BEST FLY-FISHING
IN THE COUNTRY, RAWDONS, ON THE MIDLANDS
MEANDER WAS OUR NEXT STOP ON OUR 8000
KILOMETRE ROAD TRIP. THE MEANDER IS SITUATED
ROUGHLY BETWEEN PIETERMARITZBURG IN THE
EAST AND THE DRAKENSBERG MOUNTAINS IN THE
WEST. IF YOU EVER FIND YOURSELF IN THIS AREA,
I URGE YOU TO TAKE IT SLOWLY, PACK A BACKPACK,
GO EXPLORE AND BREATHE IN THE SCENERY.
THIS IS DEFINITELY THE KIND OF PLACE WHERE
YOU SHOULD PUT YOUR FEET UP, WATCH THE
SUNSET . . . AND BRAAI SOME OF THE BEST BEEF
SOUTH AFRICA HAS TO OFFER.

Slow Braai'd
SMOKY
BEEF SHORT RIB

MARTHINUS FERN... CHEF ★ BRAAI MASTER JUDGE

YOU'LL NEED:
- short rib (15 cm x 15 cm) – ask your butcher to cut it for you

AND THEN FOR THE CURING SALT:
- a handful of fresh origanum – chopped
- a handful of fresh thyme – chopped
- 3 or 4 fresh bay leaves (use dried if you don't have fresh)
- 150 g Maldon salt
- 50 g brown sugar
- 50 g smoked paprika
- 4 cloves of fresh garlic – crushed in their skins
- sherry vinegar

FOR THE BBQ SAUCE YOU WILL NEED:
- 200 g butter
- 100 g brown sugar
- 50 ml honey
- 50 g molasses
- 200 g tomato sauce
- 20 ml mustard
- 20 ml Worcestershire sauce
- as much Tabasco as you can handle
- a squeeze of lemon juice

In a bowl, mix together the herbs, salt, sugar, paprika and whole crushed garlic, then rub the mixture generously into the ribs. Cover with cling film and leave to rest in the fridge for 5 to 6 hours. Next, you have to wipe the ribs clean to neutralise the salts so dampen a cloth with some sherry vinegar and wipe them down.

The last step before braaiing the ribs is to put them in a hot smoker and smoke using oak chips for roughly 5 minutes. Smoking the ribs will add a really *lekker* flavour. Check out page 169 to figure out how to do this if you don't already know.

Right, now you're ready for the last step. When your fire is ready and you have hot coals, grill the ribs until the outside is caramelised. Take it off the heat and out of the way of your dog who, if you have one, has been eyeballing your progress from the corner. Push the coals to the sides to form a circle (an easy way to get a slow cooking temperature) then place the ribs back on the braai. Build a feeder fire close by so you can control the temperature by adding more coals as needed. The ideal temperature for braaiing the ribs is 110-120°C. Braai for 3 to 4 hours and spend some of this time making a BBQ sauce.

Melt the butter in a pot and add the rest of the ingredients. Stir until the sugar has melted and everything has warmed up, then take it off the heat. Reheat the BBQ sauce just before the ribs are ready.

NOW YOU CAN DO ONE OF TWO THINGS.

★ When the ribs are done you can either debone them, dunk them in BBQ sauce and serve on Corn and Olive Bread (page 143), or

★ if you're like me, you can leave them on the bone, baste generously during the last 10 minutes of braai time and get your hands dirty.

When you eat ribs, you have to roll up your sleeves and put your elbows on the table. You'll know you've done a good job when you have sauce sticking to the corners of your mouth and all over your fingers (which of course you have to lick clean). *Lekker!*

HANGER STEA[K]

~

ONION RINGS

BEER BATTERED
STUFFED WITH
LIVER, BACON AN[D]

ONION

~

CRISPY CHIP[S]

BECAUSE WE WERE AT THE BOAR'S HEAD PUB IN THE MIDLANDS (AN AREA WELL KNOWN FOR SERVING SOME OF THE BEST ALES AND PUB GRUB IN THE COUNTRY) I HAVE TO INCLUDE SOME PUB BRAAI FARE.

PUB Grub

HANGER STEAK

Combine and grind the rub ingredients in a mortar and pestle or use a coffee grinder if you don't have one. Rub the steaks with the ground spices and set aside for an hour. Get your fire on a high heat, then braai for a couple of minutes a side – Roger and I agree: steaks are best served rare.

★ BEETROOT RELISH Mix all the ingredients together.

ONION RINGS

Get your braai buddy to prep the onions, while you get on with the liver. Top and tail about 6 onions and remove the outer skin. Hollow them out with a paring knife until you have only the outer layer of the onion left. Use the onion that you have removed for the Draught and Onion Liver (see below). Make a beer batter by mixing about 8 tablespoons of self-raising flour, a glug of olive oil, a pinch of salt and about half a bottle of beer (think tempura). Dunk each hollowed onion layer into the batter and deep fry in vegetable oil until golden brown. Place on a paper towel to drain.

DRAUGHT AND ONION LIVER

Put a fireproof pan on top of a braai grid over medium to hot coals. Melt the butter and sauté the chopped onions, thyme and garlic until the onions are soft. Pour the pint of Castle into the pan, add loads of Worcestershire sauce and salt and pepper to taste. Reduce the temperature of the coals to a medium heat and simmer uncovered for about 40 minutes, until it starts to thicken.

Drop the cubed beef liver into the seasoned flour and toss it around until it is well dusted. Heat another pan, add a drizzle of olive oil and sear the livers. When they're brown and caramelised (but still rare on the inside) pop them into the onion and beer sauce and simmer for another 10 minutes until cooked through.

PLACE A DEEP FRIED ONION RING ON EACH PLATE WITH A HOLLOWED END FACING UPWARDS AND STUFF WITH THE LIVER. SERVE WITH ONE HANGER STEAK, THE BEETROOT RELISH ON THE SIDE, MARTHINUS'S 'ONCE COOKED, TWICE FRIED CHIPS' (PAGE 83) AND, OF COURSE, BEER.

YOU'LL NEED:
- 4 x 300 g hanger steaks, cut about 2.5 cm thick

FOR THE RUB:
- 1 teaspoon of rock salt
- 2 teaspoons of paprika
- 1 teaspoon of garlic powder
- 1 teaspoon of whole black pepper
- a decent pinch of dried chilli
- 1 teaspoon of brown sugar

BEETROOT RELISH:
- 3 raw beetroot – peeled and julienned
- 1 pear – peeled and chopped
- a couple of cloves of garlic – mushed into a paste
- a generous glug of olive oil
- a squeeze of lemon juice
- a small handful of chopped mint
- coarse sea salt and cracked black pepper to taste

FOR THE DRAUGHT & LIVER:
- a big knob of butter
- leftover onions – roughly chopped
- a couple of sprigs of fresh thyme
- a couple of cloves of garlic – crushed and chopped
- 1 pint of Castle draught
- a generous splash of Worcestershire sauce
- salt and pepper to taste
- 1 beef liver – roughly cut into cubes
- about a cup of flour, seasoned with salt and pepper
- olive oil

THERE'S NOT A LOT IN LIFE TO BEAT THE TASTE OF STICKY, SWEET AND SMOKY CHICKEN WINGS. THE ONLY RULES ARE THAT WHEN YOU EAT THEM YOU HAVE TO END UP WITH A STICKY MESS ALL AROUND YOUR MOUTH, ON YOUR HANDS, ON YOUR BEER MUG . . . AND YOU MUST CLEAN YOUR FINGERS ON YOUR JEANS. THAT'S RIGHT . . . BECAUSE ICE-COLD BEER AND A BASKET FULL OF BBQ WINGS ARE THE BEST COMBINATION EVER. AND, NO, YOU DON'T NEED A *JAMMERLAPPIE*. YOU JUST NEED TO KNOW HOW TO LICK YOUR FINGERS CLEAN. AND THAT'S ALL I HAVE TO SAY ABOUT WINGS AND BEER, BUT I RECKON IT'S ENOUGH.

★ **PUB GRUB**

WHILE YOUR BRAAI BUDDY GETS THE FIRE STARTED, YOU CAN GET ON WITH THE SAUCE.

YOU'LL NEED:
- 2 onions – finely chopped
- a couple of cloves of crushed garlic
- 1 cup of bourbon whiskey
- coarse sea salt and cracked black pepper
- 2 cups of tomato sauce
- ⅓ cup cider vinegar
- ⅓ cup Worcestershire sauce
- ½ cup brown sugar
- a splash of Tabasco

Bourbon Basted BBQ Wings

BERTUS BASSON
CHEF
BRAAI MASTER JUDGE

Sweat off the onion and garlic, add the bourbon and cook until you're not going to pass out if you had to drink it – in other words, until all the alcohol is cooked out. Combine the boozy onions with the rest of the ingredients, taste and adjust the seasoning if you need to. Pour the sauce over about 20 chicken wings and let them marinate for as long as you can wait. Then place the wings on a grid and braai them on medium hot coals, turning and basting with the sauce as you go along. Make sure you cook them thoroughly – it should take about 20 minutes.

TAKE A COUPLE OF COLD BEERS OUT OF THE COOLER BAG, PUT THEM ON THE TABLE NEXT TO THE BASKET OF HOT WINGS, CALL YOUR FRIENDS AND DIG IN.

ROOIBOS ★ SMOKED TROUT

First up, make some mashed potatoes. I'm guessing most people know how to do this, so I'm not going to tell you. The only thing I will say is that you should add lots of butter. About 20 minutes before the mashed potatoes are ready, prep your smoker (check out page 169 for how to smoke fish with rooibos tea leaves). Melt a couple of knobs of butter and add some honey for sweetness. Baste the trout fillets with the sweet butter and when the smoker is ready, put the fillets inside. Smoke the fish for 5 to 8 minutes.

In that time, whip up a salsa verde. Take a mortar and pestle and whack in some chopped capers, parsley and fennel. Bash until fine, then add a generous drizzle of olive oil. Mix it up, add a couple of cracks of black pepper and a pinch of coarse salt. Remove the trout fillets from the smoker and place them on top of scoops of mashed potatoes. Drizzle with salsa verde.

YOU'LL NEED:

- a smoker
- mashed potatoes
- a couple of knobs of butter
- honey
- 4 fresh trout fillets
- about a tablespoon of finely chopped capers
- a small handful of chopped parsley
- a small handful of finely chopped fennel
- olive oil
- salt and pepper to taste

I'LL BE THE FIRST TO ADMIT THAT I WAS NEVER A BIG FAN OF TROUT, UNTIL I REALISED THAT THE QUALITY OF THE WATER AFFECTS THE FLAVOUR OF THE TROUT. IF YOU CATCH TROUT IN PRISTINE WATER THEY TASTE AMAZING.

Trout TAPAS

★ TROUT SASHIMI

THIS IS THE SIMPLEST OF THE TAPAS AND PROBABLY THE TASTIEST IF YOU'RE A FAN OF SUSHI. SASHIMI CAN BE ANY TYPE OF THINLY SLICED RAW FISH, AND IT IS USUALLY SERVED WITH SOYA SAUCE AND PICKLED GINGER. I LOVE THIS RECIPE BECAUSE IT'S AN INTERESTING TWIST ON TRADITIONAL SASHIMI.

YOU'LL NEED:

- fresh trout fillets – skin removed
- streaky bacon
- crème fraiche
- fresh rocket
- Kikkoman soya sauce

First things first: sharpen your knife. If you don't have a sharp knife, the trout will tear when you cut into the flesh. Next, don't make the mistake of just hacking away at it – that's not sashimi. The way you cut it will enhance the flavour and if it looks good, chances are it will taste good too.

After you've cleaned and filleted the trout (ask your fishmonger to do this for you if you don't know how), place the fillets on a clean cutting surface. Now take your (very) sharp knife and cut the trout against the grain. (It's probably a good idea to tell your friends you're about to work with a sharp knife in case they feel like giving you a fright.) The sashimi should be no more than 1 cm thick, and you simply cut it as you would a loaf of bread. As soon as you're done prepping the trout, pop it in the fridge (for no longer than 4 hours) while you get on with the rest of it.

Chop up a couple of slices of streaky bacon. Fry it in a small fireproof pan over hot coals until crispy then put it on to a paper towel to drain the excess fat.

Serve the sashimi on top of fresh rocket, with crème fraiche topped with crispy bacon bits and soya sauce on the side.

★ TROUT KEBABS

YOU'LL NEED:

- 2 fresh trout fillets
- olive oil
- 2 chillies – seeds removed and chopped
- the juice of 1 lime
- salt and pepper to taste
- cos lettuce – shredded
- bamboo kebab sticks (pre-soaked in water)

Cut the trout fillets into cubes and place in a marinade of olive oil, chilli, lime juice, salt and pepper. Leave to stand for about half an hour, then skewer the trout cubes on to the kebab sticks. Braai over medium to hot coals for about 5 minutes turning frequently and basting with the marinade until all sides are seared. (The inside of the trout should still be pink.) Serve on shredded cos lettuce.

Oopsies

ULTIMATE BRAAI RECIPE — JUSTIN BONELLO

I CALL TAPAS 'OOPSIES' BECAUSE WHEN YOU DROP YOUR FOOD ON THE FLOOR, YOU SAY 'OOPSIE', THEN YOU PICK IT UP AND POP IT IN YOUR MOUTH WHEN NO ONE IS WATCHING. (YOU KNOW ABOUT THE 5-SECOND RULE OF 'FROM THE FLOOR TO YOUR MOUTH', DON'T YOU?) YOU'LL BE GLAD TO KNOW THESE OOPSIES DON'T HAVE TO FALL ON THE FLOOR BEFORE YOU CAN EAT THEM. THERE ARE MANY STORIES ABOUT WHERE TAPAS ORIGINATED AND, AS USUAL, I'M GOING TO TELL YOU THE ONE I LIKE BEST. WAY BACK WHEN, TAPAS WERE SLICES OF SALTED MEAT (LIKE CHORIZO AND HAM) THAT WERE PLACED ON TOP OF SHERRY GLASSES IN ANDALUSIAN TAVERNS TO KEEP FRUIT FLIES OUT OF THE DRINK. THE (VERY CLEVER) TAVERN OWNERS SOON REALISED THAT THE THIRSTY TRAVELLERS GOT EVEN THIRSTIER AFTER EATING THE SLICES OF SALTY MEAT. AND SO THEY WOULD ORDER MORE DRINKS, AND THE TAVERN OWNERS STARTED CREATING DIFFERENT KINDS OF TAPAS SO THE ORDERS KEPT FLOWING.

Mix all the ingredients together, scatter over 3 of the wraps then place the remaining 3 wraps on top. Place in a sandwich grid and braai over medium coals until toasted, flip them over and toast the other side. Cut into wedges and serve with tomato chutney (page 182).

★ QUESADILLA

FOR THREE QUESADILLAS, YOU'LL NEED:
- 2 large handfuls of grated mature cheddar
- a bunch of spring onions – finely chopped
- ½ red onion – finely chopped
- 1-2 chillies – seeds removed and finely chopped
- a handful of chopped coriander
- 6 wraps

OLIVES AND CHORIZO ★

Mix together the lemon juice, rosemary, paprika and salt and pepper. Place in a small cast iron skillet and heat over medium coals, toss in the olives and chorizo and braai until the sausage turns crispy (about 20 minutes). You want the chorizo to almost dry out and the oils and flavours to be released into the olives. Serve in a bowl with toasted bruschetta.

YOU'LL NEED:
- zest and juice of 1 lemon
- 2 pinches of chopped rosemary
- a pinch of smoked paprika
- salt and pepper to taste
- a couple of handfuls of calamata olives (or use green olives if you don't like a bitter taste)
- 1 chorizo – sliced into rings

Squeeze the lemon juice into a bowl then add as much wasabi paste as you can handle. (I used about three tablespoons.) Mix it up and brush it all over the tuna. Sprinkle sesame seeds on to a clean surface then roll the tuna in them until all sides of the steak are covered with seeds. Pop on to a braai and grill over medium to hot coals, just until all sides are seared and the inside is still pink. Take the sharpest knife you have and cut the steaks into slices approximately 1 cm thick. If you don't use a sharp knife, the flesh will tear – ask any sushi chef. (Also, if you overcook the tuna, you might as well mix it into your cat's food.)

Finish by topping each slice of bruschetta with two slices of tuna steak, a couple of slices of avo, chopped spring onion, a tiny bit of salt and cracked black pepper and a shaving of pickled ginger. If there's any tuna left over, grab some soya sauce and dip and eat before anyone sees you.

★ WASABI AND SESAME CRUSTED TUNA BRUSCHETTA

First up, make your own bruschetta (page 67). If you can't be bothered, get a loaf of ciabatta and cut it into slices. Rub with raw garlic, brush lightly with olive oil and toast on the braai until crispy and golden brown.

THEN YOU'LL NEED:

- juice of ½ lemon
- wasabi paste
- tuna steaks – about ½ kg (pole caught)
- sesame seeds
- avo – finely sliced
- a couple of spring onions – chopped
- salt and cracked black pepper
- pickled ginger

ULTIMATE BRAAI RECIPE
JUSTIN BONELLO

CHILLI POPPERS ★

Cut the tops off the jalapeños, then carefully scoop out the seeds with a spoon, being careful not to tear the flesh. Next, mix the cheese, salt and pepper and then just as carefully stuff the jalapeños with the cheese. Replace the tops of the jalapeños (these are going to be the lids) and secure with a toothpick. Take a bamboo skewer and thread it through a jalapeño, so that the 'lid' is just above the skewer and the bottom half hangs down. Continue until the skewer is full, allowing some space between jalapeños. Brush with a little olive oil and place on the grid. Braai on medium coals for 4 to 6 minutes, turning frequently until the skin is slightly charred and the cheese has melted.

This recipe makes 8 chilli poppers. Double it up, because your friends will love it!

YOU'LL NEED:
- 8 medium to large pickled jalapeños
- a large handful of grated mozzarella
- a couple of buffalo mozzarella balls – torn
- salt and pepper
- toothpicks
- metal or bamboo skewers (if bamboo, soak in water beforehand)
- olive oil

Corn & Olive
BREAD

SINDI AND LETHU ARE BRILLIANT BAKERS. MARTHINUS WANTED TO ADD HIS OWN CORN BREAD IN THE BOOK AS PART OF HIS SMOKY BBQ BEEF RIB RECIPE, BUT THEN HE TASTED GAL POWER'S AND SAID I HAVE TO ADD IT. THIS REQUEST COMES FROM AN AWARD WINNING CHEF, SO YOU HAVE TO KNOW THAT IT'S A WINNER.

First up, put all your dry ingredients in a mixing bowl. Cut the butter up into chunks and, using your fingertips, rub it into the flour until it becomes crumbly. Cut the corn off the cob and roughly chop up the olives. Add them to the flour and mix everything thoroughly, then gradually add the water, kneading the dough in between splashes of water. The dough must not be too hard and should have a smooth consistency. If it is a little hard, add a little more water. Lightly coat the dough with oil (to prevent it from forming a hard crust) then put it in a big glass bowl. Cover with a damp tea towel and leave to rise in a warm sunny spot for about 45 minutes.

After time is up, sprinkle some flour on to a clean surface, remove the dough from the bowl, put it on the surface and knead it again. Grease a flat bottomed potjie, put the dough inside and let it rise for another 5 minutes. Bake the bread the same way you would bake pot bread – put it on top of a tripod over medium to hot coals and place a couple of coals on top of the lid to create an all-round oven effect. Let it bake for about 45 minutes then check to see if it's done by sticking a skewer into the centre of the bread. If the skewer comes out moist, put the bread back on to the coals and bake until cooked. Serve with Smoky BBQ Short Ribs (page 128).

YOU'LL NEED:

- 4 cups of flour
- 3 tablespoons of sugar
- 10 g instant yeast
- 40 g butter
- a mixture of Kalamata and green olives – pips removed and roughly chopped
- 1 fresh sweet corn – cut off the cob
- 375 ml lukewarm water

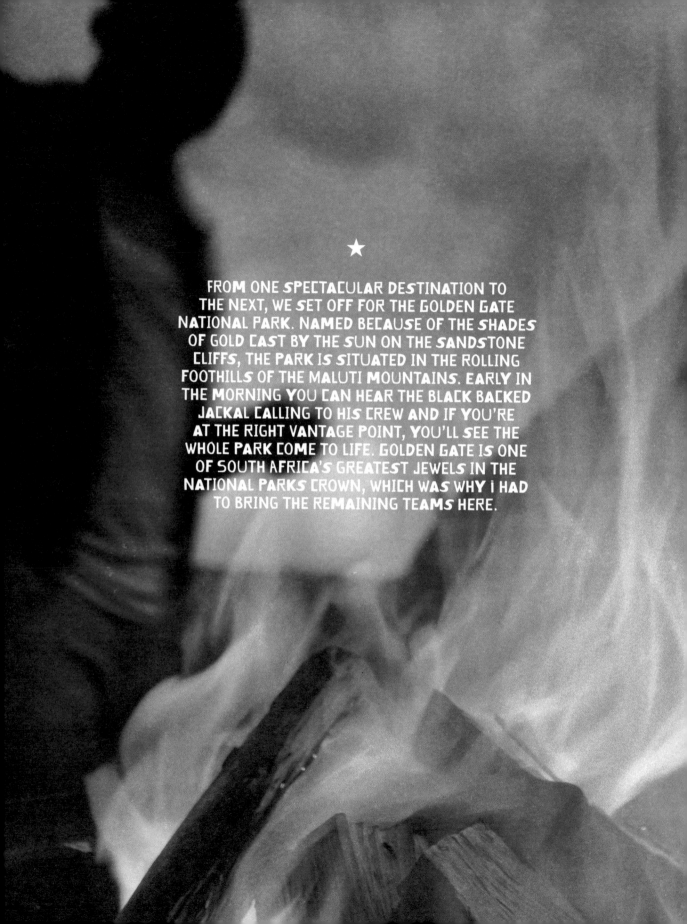

★

FROM ONE SPECTACULAR DESTINATION TO
THE NEXT, WE SET OFF FOR THE GOLDEN GATE
NATIONAL PARK. NAMED BECAUSE OF THE SHADES
OF GOLD CAST BY THE SUN ON THE SANDSTONE
CLIFFS, THE PARK IS SITUATED IN THE ROLLING
FOOTHILLS OF THE MALUTI MOUNTAINS. EARLY IN
THE MORNING YOU CAN HEAR THE BLACK BACKED
JACKAL CALLING TO HIS CREW AND IF YOU'RE
AT THE RIGHT VANTAGE POINT, YOU'LL SEE THE
WHOLE PARK COME TO LIFE. GOLDEN GATE IS ONE
OF SOUTH AFRICA'S GREATEST JEWELS IN THE
NATIONAL PARKS CROWN, WHICH WAS WHY i HAD
TO BRING THE REMAINING TEAMS HERE.

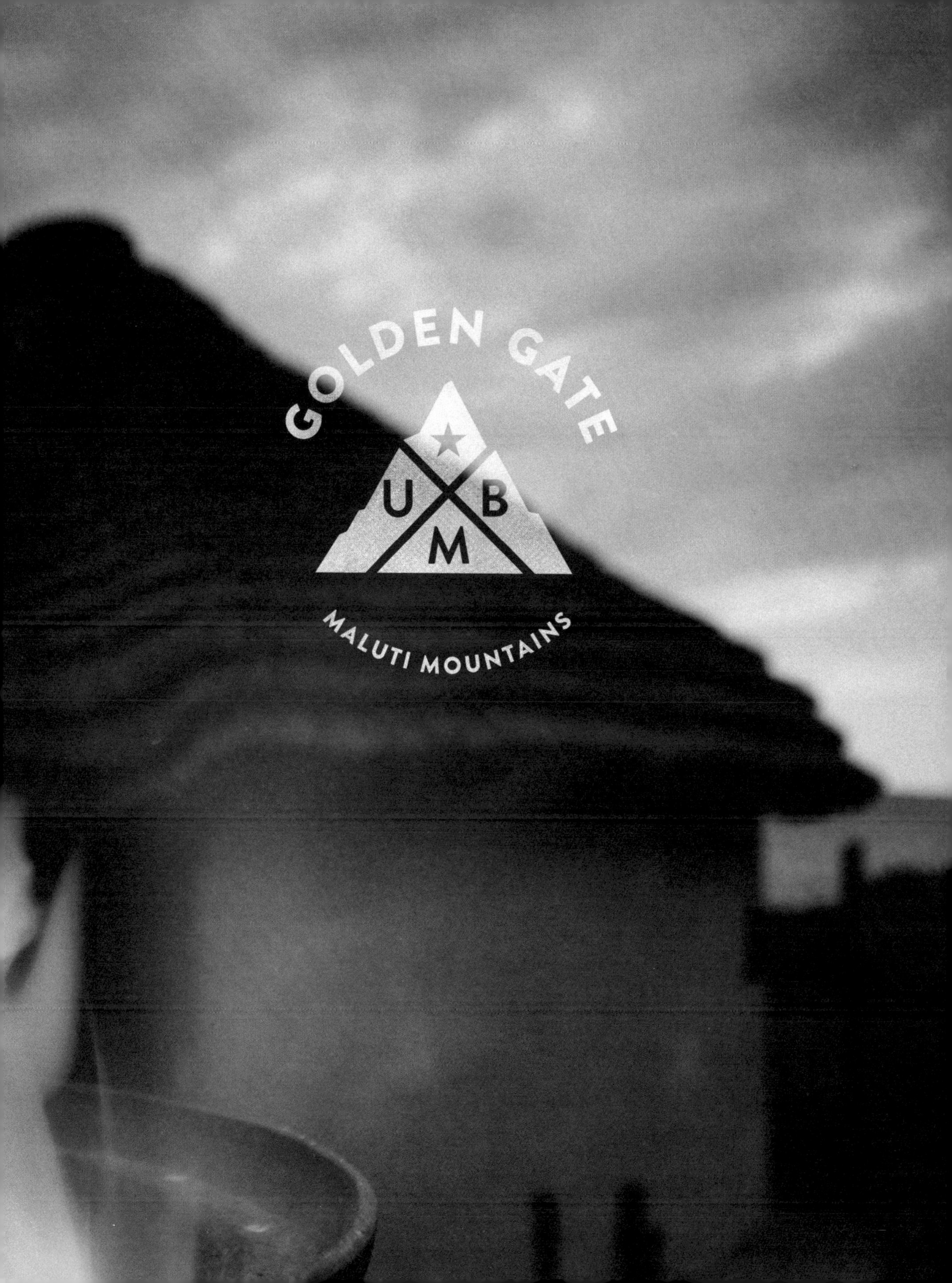
GOLDEN GATE
U B M
MALUTI MOUNTAINS

PORK
Pot Pie

THIS IS MY TAKE ON A TRADITIONAL PORK POT PIE, AND IN MY OPINION IT IS THE IDEAL WINTERTIME BRAAI DISH TO SATISFY THAT RELENTLESS HUNGER THAT COMES WITH THE COLD. YOU'LL BE HAPPY TO KNOW IT'S MUCH EASIER TO MAKE THAN THE ORIGINAL VERSION BUT IS STILL EVERY BIT AS TASTY.

First make two fires – one cooking fire and one feeder fire. Place the potjie either on a tripod or balance it on two bricks over medium to hot coals. Heat the oil and butter then add the onion and fry. Next, add the chopped bacon and just before it turns crispy, add the rosemary, garlic, celery, parsnips and carrots and fry until soft. Stir in the tomato paste and increase the heat by adding more coals from your feeder fire. Add the pork mince, salt, pepper, paprika, sage and bay leaves. When the pork mince is cooked through add the stock and the cider. Leave to simmer uncovered for about 20 minutes or until the sauce has reduced by half. Grab a spoon and taste the mince. If it lacks seasoning, now's the only time to add it, because you're about to top it with the batter.

Make the topping by simply putting all the ingredients in a bowl and whisking until smooth. Then pour the batter over the pork filling. Sprinkle with more paprika and sage leaves, then pop the potjie lid on top. Put a couple of coals on the lid to create an all-round oven effect and leave to bake until the batter is cooked and golden brown (about 40 minutes).

★

FOR THE FILLING:
- olive oil
- a knob of butter
- 1 large onion – chopped
- a couple of rashers of bacon – chopped
- a couple of sprigs of rosemary – chopped
- 2 dried bay leaves
- 2 cloves of garlic – chopped and crushed
- 3 sticks of celery – finely chopped
- 3 parsnips – peeled and chopped
- 3 carrots – peeled and chopped
- a couple of spoonfuls of tomato paste
- just under 1 kg of pork mince
- salt and pepper to taste
- a couple of pinches of paprika
- a small handful of sage leaves – chopped
- ½ cup of beef stock
- about 1 cup of apple cider

FOR THE TOPPING:
- 2 eggs
- about ¾ cup of sunflower oil
- 1 cup of milk
- 1 cup of flour
- 4 teaspoons of baking powder
- 2 teaspoons of mustard powder
- salt

OXTAIL *Potjie*

YOU'LL NEED:

- flour
- salt and pepper
- 1.5 kg oxtail
- olive oil
- 2 onions – chopped
- about 10 rashers of bacon – chopped
- about 3 celery sticks – chopped
- a couple of carrots – peeled and chopped
- a couple of sprigs of rosemary – chopped
- a couple of sprigs of thyme – chopped
- 2-3 bay leaves
- red wine
- good quality beef stock
- 1 large butternut – peeled and diced
- ½ cabbage – shredded
- 2 big handfuls of button mushrooms

THE FIRST THING YOU SHOULD KNOW ABOUT MAKING PROPER POTJIEKOS IS THAT IT'S NOTHING LIKE A STEW. WHAT I MEAN BY THIS IS THAT YOU LAYER THE FOOD ACCORDING TO COOKING TIMES AND YOU DON'T STIR THE POTJIE UNTIL THE VERY END. THE SECOND THING YOU SHOULD KNOW IS THAT A GOOD POTJIE TAKES A GOOD COUPLE OF HOURS TO PERFECT, SO START YOUR FIRE EARLY AND MAKE SURE THERE ARE ABUNDANT SNACKS TO KEEP THE HUNGRY WOLVES AT BAY. BECAUSE IT TAKES SO LONG, IT'S THE PERFECT WAY OF BRAAIING, GIVING YOU TIME TO CATCH UP WITH FRIENDS AND FAMILY, AND IT'S A GREAT EXCUSE FOR A GAME OF POKER WHILE WAITING FOR YOUR LUNCH OR DINNER.

Put about a cup of flour in a large mixing bowl and season with a decent pinch of salt and black pepper. Take a few oxtail chunks at a time and toss them around in the seasoned flour until they are well coated. Heat a drizzle of olive oil in a large potjie (nr 4 will be fine) over hot coals. Seal the floured oxtail pieces, remove them from the potjie and set aside.

Next, add the chopped onions and the bacon, sauté them for a few minutes and then add the celery, carrots, rosemary, thyme and bay leaves and fry for a couple of minutes, stirring occasionally. Put the oxtail back into the potjie, add roughly 2 cups of red wine and 2 cups of beef stock to cover the meat. Add salt and pepper taste. Simmer over medium coals for about 3 hours without stirring. Keep a feeder fire close by and keep adding coals under the potjie to maintain a consistent heat.

After about 3 hours, check the oxtail. If it's tender and falling off the bone, layer in the cubes of butternut, then the cabbage and lastly the mushrooms and simmer until the butternut is cooked (but not mushy).

 Remove the potjie from the heat, stir (for the first time) and let your friends dish up for themselves. Serve with rice, bread or mieliepap.

BOOZY
Hot Chocolate

These are the adult versions of something we all used to love as kids: hot chocolate. The difference is that they don't come with a bedtime story, but rather with fireside tales; they are not sprinkled with marshmallows and they are the perfect nightcap to enjoy under the stars around a dying fire, and not in bed. Definitely a sweet ending to any braai, with the benefits of the alcohol that will make you sleep like you used to when you were a kid. These are three of my favourites and each is enough to put four friends to sleep.

NUTTY CINNAMON MILK CHOCOLATE

- 1 litre of milk
- 1 teaspoonful of ground cinnamon
- 2 slabs of milk chocolate
- 4 tots Frangelico

Pour the milk and cinnamon into an enamel kettle and slowly bring to a simmer. Add the bashed up chocolate and stir until completely melted. Add the Frangelico and serve.

WHITE RUM AND VANILLA CHOCOLATE

- 2 vanilla pods
- 1 litre of milk
- 2 slabs of white chocolate
- 4 tots of rum, white or dark

Slice the vanilla pods in half lengthwise and scrape the seeds out with the back of a knife. Pour the milk into an enamel kettle, add the scraped out vanilla seeds and the pods and bring to a simmer. When the milk starts steaming, add the bashed up or grated white chocolate. Slowly bring the milk to the boil, giving the chocolate enough time to melt and the vanilla time to infuse the milk. As soon as the milk is hot, remove it from the heat immediately so that it doesn't burn. Add the rum, pour into mugs and watch as your friends' change from pirates into sleepy children. (If they don't, they need some more.)

DARK CHILLI AND BRANDY CHOCOLATE

- 2 chillies – sliced in half, seeds removed
- 1 litre of milk
- 2 slabs of dark chocolate (the good kind)
- 4 tots of brandy

First up, slice the chillies in half, remove the seeds and bash gently in a mortar and pestle to get the heat going. Pour the milk into an enamel kettle (the kind that's safe to put on a fire), add the bashed chilli and slowly bring to a simmer. Break the chocolate up into blocks and put it in a Ziploc bag. Then, using a rock (any kind that just happens to be lying around), bash it up until the blocks turn into crumbs. Stir the chocolate into the simmering milk and when it's melted add the brandy. (You can add more than 4 tots if you like.) Strain the chocolate milk through a sieve into mugs, taking care not to get any of the chilli slices into your friends' drinks.

Amaize
★ Balls ★

You know that tradition that mieliepap should always be served with a side of Chakalaka or relish and some boerewors? Or maybe for breakfast in the winter with loads of butter, sugar and warm milk? That's what I thought too, but then Team Foodies showed me a really interesting way of re-creating this South African favourite. And I thought you couldn't reinvent the wheel . . .!

First up, heat the milk until it's just about to boil. Add half the mielie meal to the simmering milk and stir it with a wooden spoon to prevent any lumps forming (once you have lumps in *mieliepap*, they're almost impossible to get out). Cook for about 5 minutes, or until you can taste that it's cooked through. Add the remaining mielie meal and stir it until it is pliable and similar in texture to play dough. Let it steam on a low heat for another 10 minutes. Remove it from the heat, add the salt and let it cool down. Once you can touch it without burning your hands you're ready to make the patties.

Take a ball of the mielie dough and manipulate it into the shape of a burger patty – about the diameter of a tin of shoe polish. Things are bound to get sticky so have a bowl of water handy to keep your hands moist while you work with the pap – the water will also help you to shape and smooth out the patty as you go along. Place the patties on a tray and keep them covered until you're ready to braai.

When the coals are ready place the patties on a braai grid and braai until golden brown on both sides, turning them every now and then so that they don't burn. They should be crunchy and golden brown on the outside and soft on the inside.

When cooked, serve immediately as a side dish with any braaivleis or, even better, have them for breakfast with butter, honey and cheese and a hot cup of coffee.

YOU'LL NEED:
- 1 litre of milk
- 500 g mielie meal
- a good pinch of salt

EXTRAS

If you like the idea of the patties having a cheesy crust, add about a cup of grated cheese to the cooked mieliepap dough before you start shaping the patties. If you want extra taste and texture, add a can of sweet corn to the dough. I can imagine there are endless options of what you can add. Think chillies, fresh herbs, sun dried tomatoes, Parmesan . . . I can't wait to play around with this.

Smoked
BOBOTIE WORS

MOST OF US KNOW THE HISTORY OF BOBOTIE. IT WAS BROUGHT TO OUR SHORES BY SLAVES FROM VARIOUS INDONESIAN ISLANDS AND WAS THEN ADOPTED BY THE CAPE MALAY COMMUNITY. IT WAS ORIGINALLY MADE FROM LEFTOVER SUNDAY ROASTS. BOBOTIE WAS SO POPULAR THAT IT TRAVELLED FAR AND WIDE WITH SOUTH AFRICAN SETTLERS ALL OVER AFRICA. SINCE IT IS SO RICH IN HISTORY AND CULTURE I JUST HAD TO INCLUDE THIS RECIPE. IT'S DEFINITELY A TASTE OF HOME, WITH A NICE TWIST.

FOR 3 KG OF MINCE YOU'LL NEED:

- 2.4 kg best beef
- 300 g beef fat
- 300 g pork fat

FOR THE SAUSAGE SPICE:

- 500 g raisins
- 150 ml Coca-Cola
- 250 ml non-alcoholic malt drink
- 2 bay leaves
- 1½ tablespoons of curry powder
- 1 tablespoon of mixed Italian herbs
- 1 teaspoon of turmeric
- 1 teaspoon of salt
- 1 teaspoon of black pepper
- 1 tablespoon of crushed garlic
- 1 teaspoon of coarse coriander
- 2 teaspoons of whole fennel
- 1 teaspoon of dried basil
- 1 teaspoon of dried oregano

FOR THE SMOKER:

- Lapsang Souchong tea leaves
- rooibos tea leaves
- rice

 I prefer to mince my own meat at home but you can ask your butcher to mince it for you.

The night before, when you start thinking about making bobotie wors, soak the raisins in the Coke and malt and add the bay leaves. Cover and leave in a cool spot overnight. The next morning, feed your kids, dogs and husband/wife and send them on their way. Remove the bay leaves from the liquid, put the raisins and remaining liquid into a blender and blitz it until it forms a raisin pulp. Pour the pulp over the mince, sprinkle all the dry ingredients over the top and, using your hands, thoroughly mix the mince, spices and raisin pulp together.

You have a choice now. You can either drive back to your friendly butcher and ask him to stuff the sausage casings for you, or if you know how to do it yourself, you can simply go ahead. (It will probably taste better knowing you did it.)

The thickness of the wors should be roughly the same a R5 coin. When it's done, hang it in a cold room (if you have one) or in a clean cool spot to give the flavours a chance to develop and the wors time to dry slightly. (Overnight should do the trick.) Then it's time to smoke the boerewors (no, not literally . . .). You can do this in a nifty smoker (and I don't mean your 80-year-old smoking grandmother).

Check out page 169 for smoking tips. Cold smoke the wors for 2 hours, or hot smoke for 5 minutes, then braai until just right – you know when that is! Serve with home-made Tomato Chutney (page 182) and fresh bread rolls.

Poor Man's Prawns

TEAM BRAAILIANCE AUDITIONS

★ **TEAM BRAAILIANCE** *WARNING BE CAREFUL YOU DON'T CHEW YOUR FINGERS! THESE CAN BE VERY ADDICTIVE!*

YOU'LL NEED:
- about 500 g chicken necks
- the juice of about ½ lemon
- 2 tablespoons of brown sugar

BASTING SAUCE:
- 100 g butter – melted
- a couple of shakes of your favourite braai spice

I'VE EATEN SOME PRETTY WEIRD STUFF IN MY LIFE . . . I ONCE NIBBLED ON BRAAI'D MICE ON THE BANKS OF THE PUNGWE RIVER IN MOZAMBIQUE, I'VE CLOSED MY EYES (AND CROSSED MY LEGS) WHEN I GULPED DOWN A KAROO OYSTER (AKA SHEEP KAHUNAS) AND RECENTLY HAD MY FIRST TASTE OF GOAT'S BRAIN AND OFFAL, SO WHEN I SAW CHICKEN NECKS ON THE TEAM BRAAILIANCE MENU, I WAS GAME.

I USED TO THINK THAT CHICKEN NECKS WERE ONLY GOOD FOR ADDING TO A CHICKEN STOCK OR YOUR DOG'S BOWL, BUT THEN I TASTED ONE HOT OFF THE GRID AND THOUGHT TO MYSELF: THIS IS THE BEST BRAAI SNACK EVER!

The first very important thing to know is that you shouldn't remove any excess fat from the chicken necks – it adds flavour. Put the chicken necks in a bowl and add the lemon juice and brown sugar. Massage the necks thoroughly, cover with cling wrap and leave to marinate for at least 2 hours – you could also leave it overnight. (If you'd prefer to, make an apricot marinade instead – page 180.)

As soon as the fire is ready (and your friends are starting to misbehave and are in dire need of a snack), braai the necks on hot coals. Turn them regularly and baste with the melted butter and braai spice until they are cooked through – this should take about 5 minutes depending on the heat of your coals.

Beef Intestine SOSATIES

BELIEVE IT OR NOT, THE IDEA OF COOKING INTESTINES IS NOTHING NEW. GRILLED INTESTINES IS A FAVOURITE SNACK IN MEXICO – IT'S CALLED *TRIPAS* AND MEXICANS LIKE TO SERVE IT IN TACO SHELLS (WITH A SHOT OR FOUR OF TEQUILA, I'M SURE). IN HONG KONG IT'S CALLED *ISAW* (YOU'LL PROBABLY FIND IT ON ANY STREET IN CHINA, CHINA) AND THEY LIKE TO DIP IT INTO A VINAIGRETTE OF CHILLI AND ONIONS. IN KOREA IT'S CALLED *GOBCHANG* AND THE INTESTINES ARE FLAMBÉED IN A PAN USING *SOJU* – A KOREAN DRINK THAT ALMOST TASTES LIKE VODKA (JUST SWEETER) AND GIVES THE *GOBCHANG* A UNIQUE SWEET TASTE. SO YOU SEE, INTESTINES ARE WELL TRAVELLED AND THE IDEA OF EATING THEM IS NOT AS FOREIGN AS YOU MIGHT THINK. THIS IS SOMETHING YOU'VE GOT TO TRY AT LEAST ONCE – I DARE YOU! YOU NEVER KNOW – YOU MIGHT LOVE IT! OH, AND I THINK WE SHOULD CALL OUR VERSION *KOEISTOKKE* JUST TO CONFUSE ASIAN TOURISTS.

YOU'LL NEED:

- just under 1 kg cleaned beef intestines (make sure you get the 'small' intestine, otherwise you might have a huge problem on your hands!)
- 4 tablespoons of honey
- about two tablespoons of ginger – crushed
- 2 cloves of garlic – crushed
- 1 tablespoon of olive oil
- a generous pinch of fine salt
- about a teaspoon of vinegar
- ½ a cup of sticky marinade (the barbecue sauce, page 183)
- about 1 cup water
- a packet of streaky bacon
- wooden kebab skewers

Before you start, I have one rule to add to The Black Ones' recipe – always prep and cook this outside or the smell of bubbling intestines might chase away your wife and, let's face it, you do need her in the kitchen.

First up, you have to clean the intestines thoroughly to get rid of any slime and other 'stuff' which you really don't want to eat. Even if you bought 'cleaned' ones, clean them again. Do this by first rinsing under running cold water and then separate the intestines and the fat using sharp scissors. You can rub the intestines with lemon and salt and refrigerate for a couple of hours, then rinse it under the tap again to remove any unpleasant odour. It's up to you.

When you've cleaned them, leave the intestines in a bowl of water while you make the marinade. Mix together the honey, ginger, garlic, a splash of olive oil, a good pinch of salt, a splash of vinegar and about half a cup of the home-made sticky marinade.

Next, drain as much water as possible from the intestines. Now go warn your neighbours about what you will be doing for they may wish to leave their house. Cooking this is like cooking any offal – rather do it in someone else's house or in the great outdoors so the smell can waft away in the wind.

Take a potjie (nr 4 will be fine). Place the intestines in it and pour on the marinade that you made earlier. Add to this about a cup of water and place the pot on the fire. Leave the lid slightly ajar to allow the steam to escape and to prevent it foaming at the mouth, but should that happen, simply scoop off the foam every now and then. Let the intestines simmer away for about 2½ hours, or until soft, checking every 20 minutes or so.

When cooked, remove the potjie from the fire and allow to cool. Then skewer one piece of intestine and one rasher of bacon, alternating between the two as you go along. Keep doing this until all the intestines/bacon have been used up.

Braai the sosaties on medium hot coals, turning them every minute. You'll know they're done when they have that char-grilled look. Serve with Tomato Chutney (page 182). If you don't tell your friends what they're eating my bet is that they'll never guess.

Fillet Stuffed

PORK BELLY

YOU KNOW HOW PEOPLE SAY THAT PIGS WILL EAT ANYTHING? WELL THIS RECIPE IS KIND OF LIKE THAT, BUT MORE ALONG THE LINES OF THAT OLD NURSERY SCHOOL SONG 'THERE WAS AN OLD LADY WHO SWALLOWED A FLY . . .' EXCEPT IT'S NOT AN OLD LADY, IT'S A PIG – AND IT SWALLOWED A COW . . . IN FACT, IT GULPED DOWN ONE OF THE MOST SUCCULENT PARTS OF A COW. THIS IS A PORK BELLY, STUFFED WITH A BEEF FILLET AND THEN BRAAI'D ON A ROTISSERIE. JOKES ASIDE, THIS IS SERIOUSLY *LEKKER!*

ALL YOU NEED ARE 6 INGREDIENTS

- a pork belly, with the pork loin and skin left on
- a fillet steak (the size will depend on the size of the belly because it has to fit inside it)
- peri-peri oil
- Gourmet Spice (this is only available in Pinetown, so as an alternative make your own spice with salt, black pepper, a couple of cloves of crushed garlic, paprika and coarse coriander)
- butcher's string/twine
- basting sauce of your choice

First up, trim off some of the fat from under the pork skin to make it as lean as possible. Next, using a sharp knife, score the outside skin (but don't cut through it completely) to help the crisping up process. Give the belly and fillet a good massage with peri-peri oil and be sure to wash your hands immediately afterwards. When the belly and fillet are all greased up generously rub gourmet spice all over the inside of the pork (but not the fillet).

Now comes the tricky part. Place the fillet in the middle of the pork belly and roll it up firmly. Tie the whole lot up with the butcher's string, leaving about 2 to 3 finger spaces between the knots. Put the stuffed piggy in the fridge to rest for a couple of hours.

When the pig has recovered, it's almost time for it to go on the rotisserie. Start by spiking the belly with the rotisserie pole (through the centre of the fillet) lengthwise. If you need to, secure it with wire. Let the belly rotate over medium-hot coals for about 3 hours, frequently basting the outside with your choice of basting sauce. Me? I like it spicy so I use a peri-peri sauce. The rotisserie will turn the meat around continuously so the pork will cook evenly, but the trick is to keep the fillet inside pink and medium-rare. If you get it right, the end product should be a tube of pork with beautiful crackling surrounding deliciously tender pork belly and in the centre the medium rare fillet dripping with peri-peri oil.

Serve with a variety of salads (page 97-99), sweet mustard sauce (page 182) and crisp dry white wine.

PS: If you don't have a rotisserie, you can braai the belly on a medium heat, turning it frequently, for about 3 hours.

MOVE OVER, BEAR GRYLLS . . . IN SOUTH AFRICA YOU'RE ONLY HARD-CORE ONCE YOU CAN BAKE BREAD IN THE GREAT OUTDOORS! AND WHOEVER IT WAS WHO SAID YOU CAN'T LIVE ON LOVE ALONE IS SPOT ON. YOU ALSO NEED DELICIOUS, FRESHLY BAKED BREAD. AND BEER. THIS IS COOKING SOUL'S RECIPE AND I LOVE IT, BECAUSE IT'S SO EASY TO DO AND IT'S GOT A REALLY *LEKKER* SWEETNESS TO IT. IF YOU'RE A NOVICE AT BAKING BREAD ON COALS, CHECK OUT PAGE 165 TO SEE WHAT TEMPERATURES YOUR COALS SHOULD BE FOR IDEAL BAKING.

HONEY *Bread*

Sift together the flour and salt, then add the yeast. Pour the lukewarm water, oil and honey into a separate bowl and stir until the honey has dissolved. In a mixing bowl, stir the water into the flour to form the bread dough (it should be firm but elastic). If the dough feels too wet, sprinkle some flour over the top and mix with your hands until the consistency is right. Cover with cling film and let it sleep in a nice warm spot for 30 minutes or until the dough has doubled in size.

Put the dough in the greased potjie and either place it on a tripod or balance it on two bricks over medium to hot coals. Put the lid on and place a few coals on top to create an all-round oven effect. Bake for roughly an hour or until golden brown, but be careful not to burn the bottom of the bread.

My friends from Cooking Soul say that if you want a bit of a crunch in the bread, you can add a cup of plain muesli or oats to the dough, but that's up to you.

This is the kind of bread that you eat piping hot, straight from the pot and topped with generous lashings of butter.

YOU'LL NEED:
- 3 cups white or brown flour
- 5 ml salt
- 10 g instant yeast
- 375 ml lukewarm water
- 15 ml canola oil
- 50 ml honey
- a flat-bottomed potjie (nr 3)

FLAT
Beer Bread

THIS IS ONE OF THE SIMPLEST BREADS YOU CAN MAKE ON THE FIRE, PLUS YOU'RE GOING TO USE ONE OF MY FAVOURITE INGREDIENTS – BEER! ONE IMPORTANT NOTE BEFORE YOU START: THE BREAD SHOULD BE FLAT, NOT THE BEER. JUST AS YOU WOULD NEVER DRINK FLAT BEER, YOU SHOULD NEVER COOK WITH FLAT BEER EITHER.

Sift the flour into a mixing bowl. Add the salt and pepper, parsley and yeast and then pour the beer over the whole lot. Mix everything together thoroughly with a wooden spoon. Don't add more flour – the dough is supposed to be sticky.

Grease a fireproof pan and scrape the dough on to it, spreading it out evenly. I'm going to let you try and figure out how to get it all off the spoon. Place the pan over medium hot coals and cook until the bottom of the bread has browned. Place a plate over the pan and flip it over, then place the bread back in the pan, golden side up, and cook the bottom part. When it's done keep it warm until you're ready to tuck in.

You can use this as a side for any dish, or simply serve it to your guests as a snack accompanied by different dips (see pages 184-185) to tide them over until the braai is ready.

YOU'LL NEED:

- 360 g bread flour
- salt and pepper to taste
- a small handful of fresh parsley – chopped
- ½ packet of yeast (5 g)
- 1 bottle of beer at room temperature (and a cold one for yourself)

BRAAI 101

BEFORE YOU EVEN THINK OF LIGHTING A FIRE, YOU SHOULD KNOW SOME BASIC RULES TO HELP YOU BECOME THE ULTIMATE BRAAI MASTER. BELIEVE IT OR NOT, THE ART OF MAKING BRAAIVLEIS IS MORE THAN JUST *GOOI*-ING A CHOP ON THE COALS.

I'll be the first oke to tell you that I hate braaiing with briquettes (those compressed ones). There's something I don't like about what they use to bind and reconstitute what should be wood or charcoal. When you braai on wood the smoke from the fire gives the meat a distinctive flavour and the first reason you want to braai is to give your food Umami. So you can see that what you make your braai with is just as important as what you cook on it. On that note, you should use wood that is local to your area or braai with alien vegetation whenever possible . . . have a braai, save our indigenous trees! Here are 4 of my favourites:

Other wood that also makes great coals and imparts good flavour are fruit trees. I like apple and orange.

Be careful! Just like it's great to know which types of wood to use for your coals, it's even better to know which to avoid. Poisonous woods include Oleander and Tamboti. The smoke from pine wood gives food an unpleasant, resinous flavour (and some types may be toxic) and then of course it's obvious that you can't use wood that's been treated, sealed or painted – so even if you're so desperate for a braai that you're thinking of burning the furniture . . . don't do it!

Coals

So now you've found the right type of wood, but you have no idea what to do with the coals. I think getting the right coals is probably the second biggest sign of a good braaier (the first would be that you actually managed to get the fire started). Here are the basics:

★ Once your fire is lit, it can take up to an hour for the coals to be ready, so plan ahead and start the fire before your guests arrive. (The coals of a wood fire will look grey and ashy when ready, and will probably take more or less 45 minutes to reach that stage, depending on the type of wood you're burning.)

★ A solid layer of coals will give you a very intense heat, perfect for anything that you want to braai quickly (think steaks).

★ A shallower layer of coals will have a less intense heat, which is great to braai everything else on.

★ You want the heat of the coals to reach every part of the meat, so make sure they extend a few centimetres beyond the area of the meat you're braaiing, otherwise it won't cook evenly.

Hot Enough?

Aaah. That ubiquitous question that always pops up at a braai: 'Is the fire ready yet?' This question is second only to 'Where's the ice?' Just as you would never test your bath water with both feet, you should never just chuck the meat on the grid of your braai. It's a recipe for disaster, so test the temperature first:

HOLD YOUR HAND ABOUT 10 CENTIMETRES ABOVE THE GRID THEN COUNT SLOWLY:

2 – 3 SECONDS MEANS THAT THE COALS ARE HOT

3 – 4 SECONDS MEANS THAT THE COALS ARE MEDIUM TO HOT

5 – 8 SECONDS MEANS THAT THE COALS ARE AT A MEDIUM HEAT

9 OR MORE SECONDS MEANS THAT COALS ARE AT A LOW HEAT

Perfect for steaks and chops.

Perfect for chicken and fish and to finish off steaks and chops.

Perfect for wors and baking breads and puddings.

Perfect for adding more wood and making a bonfire.

MEAT IS MEAT
AND A MAN MUST EAT!

OKAY, SO NOW YOU'VE SUCCESSFULLY MANAGED TO MAKE A FIRE, CREATE GREAT COALS FOR BRAAIING AND YOU'VE TESTED THE TEMPERATURE. WELL DONE – SO FAR YOU LOOK LIKE THE REAL DEAL. BUT THE LAST, VERY IMPORTANT THING EVERY BRAAI MASTER SHOULD KNOW IS HOW TO BRAAI DIFFERENT CUTS AND TYPES OF PROTEIN. WHEN YOU BRAAI MEAT, IT'S ALL ABOUT PRODUCING THE RIGHT TEXTURE AND FLAVOUR, AND ONCE YOU UNDERSTAND THE BASIC COOKING TIMES, YOU'LL BE ABLE TO PRODUCE A MOUTH-WATERING, TENDER AND FLAVOURSOME BRAAI EVERY TIME.

★ ★ ★ ★ ★

Look, anybody can follow a recipe, but the rule of thumb is that when you understand what happens to your food when it develops in flavour and texture, the better you'll understand how to improve your skills in the kitchen (or around the braai). This is important because when it comes to meat, it's all about getting the flavours and textures right.

SO HERE ARE 3 BASIC THINGS YOU SHOULD KNOW WHEN IT COMES TO COOKING MEAT:

★ The longer you cook meat (anything from fish, chicken, beef or lamb), the tougher or drier it will become. This happens because the heat causes the protein to coil up, which means the muscle fibres are contracting, and so the meat becomes harder and the juices are squeezed out.

★ Meat is mostly water. So, when you over-braai meat, it loses most of the moisture that's locked inside it, and that's when it will become dry and will lose some of its naturally great taste and texture.

★ The third thing you should know is that fat is a very important component in meat. When it melts as it is heated up, it flavours the meat and also acts as a lubricant, adding to the natural juiciness of the meat you're eating.

THE LESSON? DON'T EVER OVERCOOK YOUR MEAT!

IS IT DONE YET?

I'm a rare guy – I love a rare steak. But because I have to accept that not everyone has my great taste, here's a foolproof way to check how your steak is cooked:

RAW

RARE

MEDIUM RARE

MEDIUM

WELL DONE

HERE ARE SOME ESSENTIAL THINGS YOU SHOULD KNOW BEFORE JUST SLAPPING MEAT ON THE BRAAI:

Fish can be wrapped in foil, newspaper or banana leaves or it can be done straight over the coals in a sandwich grid. Braai it whichever way you like it, but please don't try and kill it again. For some reason people have a fear of eating raw fish, so they cook it to death. The result? The fish is flavourless and extremely dry and no amount of lemon juice or tartar sauce will help remedy this disaster. Rule of thumb when braaiing fish? Stick to about 20 minutes (basting regularly) then check whether it's cooked through (and still moist). If not, pop it back on the braai for a couple more minutes. With all fish, those last couple of seconds can lead to greatness or disaster.

PORK CHOPS
Coals: Hot.
Sear meat then move to medium hot coals. Braai for 10 minutes max, basting and turning often. Pork must still be slightly pink in the centre.

PORK BELLY
Check out page 160 for a delicious recipe.

WINGS
Medium to hot coals.

Marinate for at least 2 hours. Braai for roughly 20 minutes or until cooked, turning and basting regularly.

CHICKEN THIGHS, BREASTS, DRUMSTICKS AND OTHER PARTS
Medium to hot coals.

Marinate for at least 2 hours or use a dry rub. Braai for about 40 minutes, turning and basting regularly.

BONELESS CHICKEN BREAST
Medium to hot coals.

Marinate for a couple of hours before braaiing. Braai for about 10 to 15 minutes, basting and turning regularly to keep it moist.

TIPS
Braai chicken with the skin on, it helps to keep in the moisture. If you don't like chicken skin, just remove it before eating.

Trim any excess fat from chicken pieces.

You'll know the chicken is cooked through when you pierce the flesh with a skewer and the juices run clear.

Check out the lamb chart on page 65 and page 64 for some *lekker* lamb recipe ideas.

THE PERFECT STEAK
Direct heat
Coals: Hot
Sear the steak on all sides to seal it, then take it off the heat. Put it back on the braai and cook it to your friends' taste only when you're ready to serve. Pop the steak back on to the now medium to hot coals, and braai to the desired degree of done-ness. For medium rare, braai for about 5 to 8 minutes a side (max), depending on the thickness of the steak. Check out the hand test sketch for a guide to how you know the meat is done. Remember, it's easier to undercook it and then cook it some more, than to overcook it because you can't reverse the process.

TIPS
Buy good quality meat. Bring steak to room temperature and pat dry with paper towel before seasoning and putting it on the braai.

After cooking, let it rest for at least 5 minutes before slicing, to allow the juices to redistribute evenly and give you a juicier steak.

When turning a steak around on the braai, don't use a fork, knife or any other sharp object you have managed to get your hands on. When you do this, you're essentially piercing holes into the meat, and this means that it is losing moisture, and that means that even if you braai'd the steak perfectly, it could be dry. Use braai tongs. Seriously, they exist for a very good reason. Or do it like me, and just use your fingers.

★

TRADITIONAL CRAFTS (THINK WINE, BEER AND BILTONG
MAKING, BREAD BAKING, CARPENTRY AND SO ON) ARE TODAY
INCREASINGLY RETURNING TO THE HOME SPACE. THE SAME CAN
BE SAID ABOUT SMOKING MEAT OR FISH, AND IT'S BOUND TO
BRING OUT THE SUPER (BRAAI) HERO IN YOU – IF YOU GET IT
RIGHT. ONCE YOU'VE MASTERED THE ART OF SMOKING IT MEANS
YOU GET TO CONTROL THE SALTINESS, FLAVOUR AND SMOKE
LEVELS IN WHATEVER FOOD YOU'RE SMOKING, AND THE BEST
PART IS THAT YOU'LL GET TO EAT SOMETHING JUST THE WAY YOU
LIKE IT. IF YOU'RE A NOVICE, THERE'S BOUND TO BE SOME TRIAL
AND ERROR ALONG THE WAY, BUT THAT'S ONLY NATURAL WHEN
YOU'RE LEARNING SOMETHING NEW.

THIS IS A
Smoking Area

BRAAI TIME
METHODS

TURNING YOUR KETTLE BRAAI INTO A SMOKER

Kill the fire inside the kettle braai by putting the lid on and closing the air intakes. When the fire's mellowed out, put whatever you're about to smoke on top of the grid. Push the coals to either side of the braai and scatter a small handful of smoking chips over them, put the lid back on, open the air intakes and let the meat smoke. The wood chips will ignite quickly because of the heat of the coals, but if you want maximum smoke levels, soak the chips in water for about an hour before putting them on top of the coals. This also stops the temperature of the coals from flaring up. If you want to add subtle flavours to your food, soak the chips in beer or any flavoured liquid instead of water.

The aromas of wood chips vary, depending on the type of tree the wood comes from. Here's a basic guideline to get you started, but I still prefer to use a light smoke because sometimes heavy smoke can overpower the flavour of the actual meat.

HEAVY SMOKE
Great For Pork Or Beef
HICKORY

MEDIUM SMOKE
Ideal For Poultry, Game and Fish
OAK

SWEET SMOKE
Ideal For Poultry, Fish and Other Seafood
APPLE

EASY SMOKING (FISH)
YOU'LL NEED:

- a smoking dish – the bottom half of an ordinary deep roasting pan is fine
- tin foil – enough to line the bottom of the pan and trap the smoke inside it
- a flat wire grid that fits into the pan

Simply line the bottom of the pan with the foil, shiny side up, then sprinkle rooibos tea leaves evenly over the bottom of the pan.

Place the seasoned fish (skin side down, if you choose to leave it on) on top of the wire grid and fit this into the pan. Take some foil and cover the pan (shiny side down) to seal. Make sure that there are no gaps where the smoke might escape. Place the roasting tin over hot coals for roughly 5 to 10 minutes, depending on the size of the fish.

★

HOT SMOKING
This is probably the method that everyone knows and uses because it's the fastest way to smoke meat. When you hot smoke meat, you're essentially smoking and cooking the meat simultaneously, because the hot smoked items are placed in the same enclosure that is heated by the fire. The hot smoking process could take anything from a couple of minutes to a couple of hours – depending on the type of meat you're smoking, the size of your smoker and whether you want it to be completely cooked through or just sealed on the outside. You can use it for meat, fish or chicken and the temperatures reached when hot smoking will kill any microbes present in the food. You can also do veggies to give them a nice smoky flavour.

★

COLD SMOKING
With cold smoking all you're essentially doing is flavouring and curing the meat, and this process can take hours. This is because the smoke passes by the food that is placed in an area separate from the fire. Generally the food remains at room temperature during the smoking process so no cooking takes place. The inside texture of the food isn't affected and nor are there any microbes present in the meat or fish. For this reason cold smoking has traditionally been combined with salt curing, particularly in foods like cheeses, bacon and cold-smoked fish like trout.

Build Your Own
SMOKER

★ THE KASSIE

YOU'LL NEED:

- 1 x 25 litre brand new and empty paint drum with lid (make sure it isn't plastic coated, for obvious reasons)
- 1 x wire rack that will fit sideways into the paint drum
- wood chips for smoking
- a braai

BRAAI TIME ★ METHODS

To smoke fish or meat, all you need is a source of heat and a sealable container of some kind – like the kassie.

Scatter about 2 to 3 tablespoons of wood chips across the bottom of the kassie. Oak or fruit wood works well with fish, and a generous sprinkle of rooibos tea leaves is great for trout. You can get wood chips from most hardware and camping stores, and one bag will last forever. My advice for smoking fish? Make sure it's not moist, so before smoking it, fillet the fish, hang it in the wind for about half an hour or until tacky and then smoke it. If the fish is moist, all the smoky flavours will go into the moisture and not the fish.

Start a fire in a braai, then when the coals are ready (medium to hot) place the kassie on its belly, straight on the coals. Seal the opening with the paint drum lid. Smoke for about 5 minutes onwards, depending on the size of the fish.

PS: If you've over-smoked the fish, simply wipe it with a damp cloth to get rid of some of the smokiness.

Braai Time

SPIT BRAAI

THINK THAT BUILDING YOUR OWN SPIT IS IMPOSSIBLE? THINK AGAIN. THIS SPIT WAS DESIGNED AND MADE BY MY FRIEND GARETH BEAUMONT AND ME IN JUST 10 MINUTES ON HIS FATHER-IN-LAW'S FARM GALILEO IN GRABOUW.

YOU WILL NEED:

- 2 x uprights of hollow square steel with a 4 cm diameter – 100 cm long.
- 1 x spit pole made from hollow square steel with a 2 cm diameter – 200 cm long
- 2 x crosspieces of solid round steel with a 0.5 cm diameter – 20 cm long
- 2 x butcher hooks (or bend your own from pieces of steel)
- small roll galvanised wire with a 1.25 mm gauge

STEP 1
Drill three holes 5 cm apart and 5 cm from the top of the 4 cm diameter uprights, big enough to fit your butcher hooks.

STEP 2
Dig a pit about 20 cm deep and 50 cm by 180 cm wide and long.

STEP 3
Using a mallet (or a big piece of wood) hammer the 4 cm diameter steel uprights into the ground on either side of your pit until only half the upright is sticking out. Remember, the holes must face the length of the pit, and be on the same side.

STEP 4
Insert butcher hooks into the drilled holes. These holes are used to adjust the height of the lamb above the fire. Up is cooler. Down is hotter.

HOW TO ATTACH A LAMB (OR ANY OTHER ANIMAL)

STEP 1
Push spit pole through the lamb's rear end until the lamb is centred on the pole.

STEP 2
Secure two crosspieces in front of chest, and behind back legs with the galvanised wire.

STEP 3
Secure two legs together (intertwined) through the hooks with the galvanised wire. Repeat for both front and rear legs.

STEP 4
Poke wire through the back of the lamb to secure the spine to the spit pole in four to five places from the neck to the pelvis and twist tight with a pair of pliers.

Once attached, check again and remove any fat without damaging the meat.

POTJIE BASICS

IF YOU TAKE GOOD CARE OF YOUR POTJIE POT IT WILL BE AROUND FOR YEARS. AFTER USING IT, WASH IT THOROUGHLY WITH SOAPY WATER, RINSE AND DRY. FINISH OFF BY RUBBING A BIT OF VEGETABLE OIL ON THE INSIDE, WHICH HELPS TO PREVENT RUSTING.

★ When using a flat bottomed potjie always put it on a tripod or balance it on two bricks. Never just put it straight on top of hot coals. That's a recipe for disaster.

★ Layer the food: first the stuff that will take the longest to cook to the food that has the shortest cooking time.

★ Once it's simmering away, don't stir it.

★ Keep a feeder fire close by so that you can maintain a consistent heat.

★ Start the potjie early – unless you have forgiving friends who don't mind waiting for hours on end to get fed.

A NUMBER WHAT NOW?

Potjie pot sizes can be a little daunting, especially if you don't know how many mouths it will feed. Never fear. Here's the answer:

 POTJIE NO. **1** FEEDS 4*

POTJIE NO. **2** FEEDS 8*

 POTJIE NO. **3** FEEDS 12*

POTJIE NO. **4** FEEDS 16*

 POTJIE NO. **6** FEEDS 22*

 POTJIE NO. **8** FEEDS 30*

 POTJIE NO. **10** FEEDS 46*

 POTJIE NO. **14** FEEDS 58*

 POTJIE NO. **20** FEEDS 94*

 POTJIE NO. **25** AN ENTIRE VILLAGE*

People it will feed (with side dishes)

Pit Oven

THE IDEA BEHIND COOKING IN A PIT OVEN IS THAT WHATEVER YOU'VE PUT INSIDE WILL COOK VERY SLOWLY – THINK OF IT AS AN UNDERGROUND PRESSURE COOKER. THE GREATEST THING ABOUT IT? IT'S PRETTY MUCH IMPOSSIBLE TO BURN YOUR FOOD. PIT OVEN COOKING IS NOTHING MORE THAN A SLOW, EVEN RELEASE OF HEAT WITHIN A SEALED HOLE, AND BECAUSE THERE ARE NO FLAMES TO WORRY ABOUT IT'S IMPOSSIBLE TO BURN YOUR FOOD. SIMPLY PUT: THIS IS NATURE'S PRESSURE COOKER AND PLEASE REMEMBER THAT IT IS A STEAMER.

First things first. Go scrounge for igneous rocks, and igneous rocks only (these are the same ones that are used in saunas). If you use any other type of rock it will explode and if you're actually making a pit oven braai it means you're nowhere near a hospital. You can test if the rocks you've collected are igneous if you take two, bash them together and your ears start ringing. But take heed, this is not always an idiot-proof method of checking for igneous rocks.

So once you've gathered a whole lot of bigger-than-your-fist igneous rocks, wipe the sweat off your brow and dig a hole roughly three times bigger than the food you're going to put inside. Pack the rocks to one side then make a huge fire (somewhere on the ground where you won't burn down trees) next to the hole you've just dug. Once your fire is blazing, put the rocks around it to let them heat up.

TO COOK IN THE PIT

★ After a while, take a rock out of the fire and splash some water on to it. If the water evaporates immediately, it's hot enough. (If not, put it back next to the fire and test again about 20 minutes later.)

★ Now pack the hot rocks inside the hole (at the bottom and the sides). Don't try to pick them up with your bare hands, use tongs for this.

★ Put loads and loads of fresh herbs that you think will complement the dish you're making straight on top of the rocks.

★ Wrap whatever you're cooking in banana leaves (you can do vegetable parcels, chicken or even bigger cuts of meat) and place it on top of the herbs. (If you've become a pit oven pro, try cooking a whole lamb or even a pig.)

★ Cover with more herbs, any remaining banana leaves and pile on the hot rocks. Cover with an old towel or piece of fabric to keep the sand out.

★ Fill the hole with sand and find something to mark the spot . . . unless you want to play hide and seek later.

ESTIMATED COOKING TIMES VARY AND DEPEND ON MANY FACTORS.

Here's the basic gist of it, although it's better to cook for longer if you're unsure. Your food won't burn, but once you've opened up the pit oven, it's a mission to close it again.

- A vegetable parcel: between 1½ to 2 hours
- A whole chicken: between 2 to 3 hours
- A whole pig: between 6 to 8 hours
- A whole lamb: between 8 to 10 hours

MARINADES

JUST AS SOME KIDS LIKE TO BE TUCKED UP IN BED AT NIGHT AND HEAR A BEDTIME STORY (TO ENSURE A GOOD NIGHT'S SLEEP AND BEST BEHAVIOUR THE NEXT DAY), CERTAIN TYPES OF MEAT NEED TO SLEEP IN A MARINADE FOR THEM TO BEHAVE IN THE RIGHT WAY WHEN YOU BRAAI THEM.

YOU MARINATE MEAT FOR TWO REASONS. ONE, TO TENDERISE TOUGHER CUTS OF MEAT AND, TWO, WHEN YOU USE THE RIGHT TYPE OF MARINADE WITH THE RIGHT CUT OF MEAT IT ENHANCES ALL THOSE *LEKKER* NATURAL FLAVOURS. PAPAYA, BUTTERMILK, YOGHURT AND BEER ARE ALL NATURAL TENDERISERS, SO KEEP THAT IN MIND NEXT TIME YOU'RE STUCK WITH A TOUGH PIECE OF MEAT. IF YOU WANT A STICKY, CARAMELISED EFFECT (THINK CHICKEN WINGS AND RIBS), USE SOMETHING TO SWEETEN UP THE MARINADE, LIKE HONEY AND BROWN SUGAR, BUT ONLY BASTE THE MEAT WITH IT TOWARDS THE END OF THE BRAAIING TIME OTHERWISE IT WILL BURN.

I THINK A MARINADE WORKS BEST WHEN THE MEAT RESTS IN IT OVERNIGHT, BUT IT'S REALLY UP TO YOU. THE ONLY RULE IS THAT YOU SHOULDN'T MARINATE YOUR MEAT FOR MORE THAN 48 HOURS, UNLESS YOU VACUUM SEAL IT. THESE ARE THREE OF MY FAVOURITES:

FRESH CORIANDER, HERB AND HONEY FOR LAMB

Put all the ingredients into a blender and blitz until smooth. If you don't have a blender, bash everything up in your mortar and pestle. Rub the marinade all over the lamb, cover with cling wrap and refrigerate for 24 hours.

YOU'LL NEED:

- loads of fresh garlic
- a chunk of fresh ginger
  – peeled and roughly chopped
- a couple of chillies
  (if you like it hot, keep the seeds;
  if not, remove them)
- juice of 1 lemon
- zest of ½ lemon
- a couple of splashes of Kikkoman
  soya sauce
- a splash of olive oil
- about 3 tablespoons of honey
  or brown sugar
- a small handful of fresh parsley – chopped
- a small handful of fresh mint – chopped
- a handful of fresh coriander – chopped
- salt and black pepper

ULTIMATE BRAAI RECIPE
JUSTIN BONELLO

APRICOT AND ROSEMARY FOR CHICKEN

Remove the leaves from the rosemary sprigs, then mix them with all the other ingredients and pour over the chicken. Cover and leave in the fridge to marinate while you sleep.

YOU'LL NEED:

- a couple of sprigs of rosemary
- a couple of dollops of apricot jam (the kind you get from your *ouma* at Christmas)
- two red chillies – seeds removed and chopped
- a generous squeeze of honey
- a good drizzle of olive oil
- a big chunk of fresh ginger – crushed and chopped
- juice of 1 lemon
- about 2 tablespoons of wholegrain mustard
- a splash of beer
- salt and black pepper

APPLE CIDER AND GINGER FOR PORK

Put all the ingredients in a pot over medium-hot coals. Bring it to the boil, reduce the heat by scraping some of the coals to one side. Cover the pot and let the marinade simmer for about 10 minutes. Take it off the braai and let it cool completely. Then pour it over the pork, cover it and leave in the fridge overnight.

YOU'LL NEED:

- a bottle of apple cider (not the vinegar – the drink!)
- a couple of star anise
- a couple of dried bay leaves
- 1 onion – sliced into rings
- a chunk of fresh ginger – peeled and grated
- coarse sea salt and black pepper
- a couple of tablespoons of preserved ginger (the kind you would eat with sushi – you'll find it at any Asian supermarket)
- a couple of tablespoons of the preserved ginger juice
- a drizzle of honey

Sauce -o- Magic

Jar-O-Mustard

YOU'LL NEED: 8 teaspoons of mustard powder + 4 tablespoons of sugar + a pinch of salt + 4 tablespoons of boiling water + 4 egg yolks + 2 tablespoons of vinegar

Make this sauce once and you'll never look back. This is a sweet mustard with a nice tang that you can use to zhoozsh up boerie rolls, burgers, sandwiches or pork dishes. Mix together the mustard powder, sugar, salt and boiling water. In a separate bowl whisk the egg yolks and vinegar, then combine the mustard and egg mixture in a glass or tin bowl. Bring a pot of water to the boil (filled about half way) and balance the glass bowl on top. If the mixture gets too hot, the eggs might scramble, so work carefully (and remove it from the heat and keep stirring if you need to stop it from scrambling). Stir until the sauce is thick, then mix in a tablespoon of butter while the mustard is still warm. Scoop it into a nifty sterilised jar and store away in your fridge. It will keep for a couple of weeks . . . but then again, it's so *lekker* it might not.

Pot-O-Chutney

YOU'LL NEED: almost 1 kg baby tomatoes (halved and with skins on) + olive oil + balsamic vinegar + cracked black pepper + fresh basil leaves + 1 onion – finely chopped + 3 red chillies – seeds removed and finely chopped + a couple of cloves of garlic – crushed and chopped + coarse sea salt to taste + a chunk of ginger – peeled and grated + 2-3 tablespoons of brown sugar

This is a chunky and sweet tomato chutney. Preheat the oven to 200°C. Put the sliced baby tomatoes on a roasting tray (flesh side up) and drizzle with olive oil and a couple of splashes of balsamic vinegar. Sprinkle with black pepper and fresh basil leaves and pop it in the oven. Bake until the tomatoes are soft and juicy. While the tomatoes are on the go, grab a non-stick pan, add a splash of olive oil, and then the chopped onion, chilli and garlic and fry until the onion is soft. When the tomatoes are cooked (and cooled down) chop them up and add to the onion mixture. Now add about ½ cup of balsamic vinegar, crushed sea salt, the ginger and about 2-3 tablespoons of brown sugar. Simmer for 15 minutes until thickened. Allow to cool and then scoop it into jars and store in your fridge. The longer the chutney stands for, the more the flavour will develop.

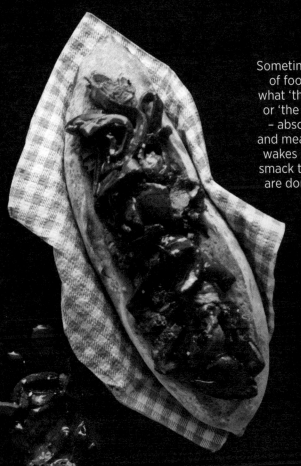

★

Sometimes the secret to the perfect plate of food is the sauce. Sauce is to meat what 'the little black dress' is to a woman or 'the perfect biltong knife' is to a man – absolutely essential. The right sauce and meat combination enhances flavours, wakes up the taste buds and makes lips smack together in surprise. Most of these are done in the kitchen, but they are an essential part of the braai.

Boozy Sauce

YOU'LL NEED: a knob of butter + 1 onion – chopped + a couple of cloves of garlic – chopped + two cups of easy drinking red wine (one for the sauce and one for yourself) + 150 ml good quality beef stock + 50 ml cream + salt and black pepper

This is a great sauce to serve with venison or any red meat. Plus it's a great excuse to have a glass of red wine before lunchtime. Melt the butter in a non-stick frying pan and then drop in the onion. Cook the onion slowly on a low heat until soft and buttery. Next add the garlic, stir and then pour in the red wine. Let the sauce simmer uncovered until it's reduced by half, then add the beef stock and reduce again. Lastly, add the cream, let it bubble away gently for about 5 minutes, then add salt and pepper to taste. Serve warm, either drizzled over a decent steak or any kind of venison, or put it on the table and let your friends help themselves. (If they're like my friends, one of them will probably end up licking out the bowl.)

Barbecue Sauce

YOU'LL NEED: 30 ml chutney + 30 ml tomato sauce + 15 ml Worcestershire sauce + 15 ml canola oil + 5 ml vinegar + 2 ml salt + 2 ml black pepper + 5 ml mustard powder + 5 ml mixed herbs

This is a great basting sauce (think steaks, burgers, ribs and wings). It's so simple! I urge you to make your own and keep it in a sealed bottle in your fridge.

Simply mix all the ingredients together, pour it into a re-sealable glass bottle and you're done.

Versatile
DIPS

BUTTERNUT HUMMUS

Peel the butternut and cut it into cubes. Place on a greased roasting tin, add the whole, peeled garlic cloves and chilli flakes and roast until soft. Remove from the oven and let it cool down. Drain the chickpeas, but keep the juice aside. Put the chickpeas in a blender, add the chopped garlic, tahini paste, lemon juice, olive oil and a splash of the chickpea juice and blend until smooth. Add the butternut and a pinch each of turmeric, cumin and cayenne pepper. Blend again and taste. If it's too bland adjust the seasoning until it's to your liking and if it's too thick add more olive oil. Scoop into dipping bowls and refrigerate until you serve it.

YOU'LL NEED:
- 1 medium-sized butternut (300 g)
- 3 cloves of garlic – peeled but left whole
- a couple of pinches of chilli flakes
- 1 tin chickpeas
- 2 cloves of garlic – chopped
- 2 tablespoons of tahini paste
- a good squeeze of lemon juice
- a drizzle of olive oil
- a splash of the chickpea juice
- a pinch each of turmeric, cumin and cayenne pepper
- sea salt

GONE ARE THE DAYS OF MAKING TACKY DIPS WITH CREAM CHEESE AND MSG. DON'T JUST MAKE THE KIND OF DIP THAT YOU SERVE WITH GREASY CHIPS TO TIDE YOU OVER WHILE YOU WATCH THE RUGBY WITH YOUR MATES. THESE ARE THE TYPES OF DIP THAT YOU CAN SERVE WITH FRESHLY BAKED BREAD, ON TOP OF BRAAI'D FISH, CHICKEN OR MEAT – THE POSSIBILITIES ARE ENDLESS. DON'T BE SURPRISED IF YOU FIND YOURSELF LICKING OUT THE BOWL JUST TO MAKE SURE NONE OF IT GOES TO WASTE!

BEETROOT HUMMUS

YOU'LL NEED:

- 6 baby beets
- 3 cloves of garlic – peeled but left whole
- a drizzle of olive oil
- a drizzle of balsamic vinegar
- 1 tin chickpeas
- 2 cloves of garlic – chopped
- 2 tablespoons of tahini paste
- a splash of the chickpea juice
- a good squeeze of lemon juice
- sea salt

Peel the baby beets, add the whole garlic cloves, drizzle with olive oil and balsamic vinegar and roast until soft. Remove from the oven and allow to cool.

Drain the chickpeas, but keep the juice aside. Put the chickpeas in a blender; add the chopped garlic, tahini paste, lemon juice, a splash of olive oil, a splash of the chickpea juice, the baby beetroot and whole roasted garlic, then blend until smooth. If it's too thick add another drizzle of olive oil and adjust the seasoning to your liking.

WARM ARTICHOKE DIP

YOU'LL NEED:

- a can of artichokes, drained and chopped
- a cup of mayonnaise
- a cup of grated parmesan
- a pinch of garlic salt

Mix all the ingredients together, put them in a casserole and bake in a preheated oven at 175°C for about 30 minutes or until bubbling. This is seriously *lekker* with braai'd fish!

FETA, PEA AND MINT DIP

YOU'LL NEED:

- 1 cup of frozen peas
- 200 g feta
- a splash of milk or olive oil
- a heaped teaspoon of mint jelly
- a small handful of fresh mint leaves

Pour boiling water over the frozen peas, leave for a couple of seconds and then drain. Mix all the ingredients together and blend until smooth. This is delicious with lamb!

SMOKY BRINJAL DIP

YOU'LL NEED:

- 2 large brinjals
- 100 ml plain yoghurt
- juice of ½ lemon
- 1 clove of garlic – crushed
- 1 green chilli – chopped (use more if you like spicy food)
- about 6 calamata olives – pitted and chopped
- a pinch of ground coriander
- olive oil
- salt and cracked black pepper
- poppadoms

To save the brinjal's bad reputation I'm giving you Fat Cow's recipe for eggplant dip which you can serve with poppadoms as a braai snack. Fat Cow served it cold, but I prefer it warm – you can decide for yourself.

Fire up the braai, and while the coals are still very hot, braai the brinjals whole until the skin is blackened and the flesh is soft. Leave to cool down and then peel off the charred skin and chop up the flesh. Mix with the yoghurt, lemon juice, crushed garlic, chopped chilli, olives, coriander and a generous splash of olive oil. Taste before seasoning with sea salt and cracked black pepper. Mix it until it's smooth, scoop into dipping bowls and drizzle with more olive oil and lemon juice.

Place the uncooked poppadoms on a braai grid over hot coals, and watch as they contort and blister. You need to braai them for only 30 seconds a side, and if you are easily distracted, rather do them one at a time to avoid burning them. The poppadoms should be crispy and lightly charred when done. Alternatively, serve the dip with lightly salted crisps or with fire-baked bruschetta (page 67).

BRAAI tongs

TO TURN THE MEAT...UNLESS YOU HAVE
NO FEELING IN YOUR HANDS

FILLETING KNIFE

TO FILLET THAT FISH
YOU JUST CAUGHT

KNIFE SHARPENER

EVERY BRAAI MASTER SHOULD HAVE ONE

SKEWERS

MAKE KEBABS
(OR IF YOU HAVE
ENOUGH, PLAY
PICK-UP-STICKS)

BASTING BRUSH

TO 'PAINT' FLAVOUR ONTO MEAT

JAFFLE IRON

TO MAKE *LEKKER* SNACKWICHES
WHEN YOU'RE CAMPING

MEAT CLEAVER
WORK YOUR OWN MEAT – BUTCHER STYLE!

BRAAI TOOLS
U B M
THE ULTIMATE BRAAI MASTER

SHARP KNIFE
ESSENTIAL FOR EVERY BRAAI

SCALING KNIFE
TO REMOVE SCALES OFF THE SKIN OF FISH.. NOT SO *LEKKER* TO EAT.

MEAT Tenderising Mallet
IT LOOKS LIKE A HAMMER FOR A REASON...

Meat THERMOMETER
FANCY TOOL TO USE TO CHECK IF THE INSIDE OF YOUR MEAT IS COOKED YET

BRAAI GRID
AWAYS HANDY IF YOU HAVE A BRAAI

BEER CAPS
WHAT'S A BRAAI WITHOUT A *KUIER*?

THANKS

My thanks must start with all the guys and girls, the South Africans who gather round a fire whenever they can to *kuier*. You were the inspiration I needed to get this off the ground . . . and on to the coals.

TO ALL THE TEAMS:

2M (Sebastian Matroos and Dumisani Malaza), Umlilo (Annerie Burger and Martyn Schickerling), Stoned Olives (Ronel Theron and Billy Stanley), Rust n Dust (Greg Gilowey and Karl Tessendorf), Popeye and Olive (Roxanne van Breda and Barry Davis), Hout Cuisine (Oscar and Christopher Foulkes), Green Okes (Tshepo Nkosi and Modise Khoabane), The Green Feet Team (Tinus Els and Lekitlane Mokiti), Gal Power (Sindi Manthata and Lethu Ncengwa), Fat Cow (Warwick Thomas and Dayle Dohne), Chi Town Braaisters (Frank Dunn and Claire Walker), Cooking Soul (Nqobani and Mbuso Mlagisi), Coal Shoulder (Roger Harris and Lee Jennery), Who Dares Wins (Laertes (Tubby) Melidonis and Elaine Ensor Smith), Which Way Braai Chicks (JanieB Smit and Maudie Bleach). Thank you for being part of the inaugural Ultimate Braai Master!

Thank you to my incredibly patient wife Eugenie. Then of course, as always, my mom Jeanne, sons Dan and Samuel, my dad Carlos and sister Tanya and her family.

Then to my crazy circus family at Cooked: my partner Peter Gird, Sunel Haasbroek, Wesley Volschenk, Raylene Stevens, Megan Bryan, Lara Black, Jei Lindeque, Kirsty Abbey, Mishal Fortune, Karla Peetz, Mark Samuels, Rugayah Essop, Thomene Dilley, Herman Wärnich, Marlese Lenhoff, Stephen Kramer, Grant Poole, Robert Whitehead, Taz Wilde, Brian Waters, Charl Cater, Zahir Isaacs, Roshni Haraldsen, Darren Illet, Brad Theron, Ian Belknap, JB Guelord-Ngandu Bilamba, Llewellyn Rice, Laura Barcley, Tazneem Ozman, Georgie Caldow, Matthew Abraham and Robyn Leigh Elford. The thanks offered here cannot adequately express my gratitude to all of you.

I'm not sure how to thank Bertus Basson and Marthinus Ferreira but I now consider you both lifetime friends who are always welcome around my fire . . . does that get me a permanent table at Overture and DW eleven-13?

Then, in no particular order, thanks to Gareth Beaumont, Grant Spooner, Mike Nyembe, Travis Nel, Lee Jackson, Josh Yon, Sebastien Lallemand, Luke Longmore, Johann Joubert, Yvonne Short (the miracle worker and magician of finding the impossible), Jenna Short,

Warren Cupido, Rob Nel, Ewan and Monica Rosie, Rebecca Brett, Pieter Bosman, Lala du Plessis, Aboubakar Toure, Vuyo Carlos Nyamaza, Darryn Welman, Chris Teodorczuk, Matthew O'Connor, Dean Engela, Brian Askew, Giles Harris, Olof Berg, Lawrence Nhweni, Steve Chembe and the team at Tenacity – Jamez Mentz, Annabel Yeaman, Terri-Mae Alexander. Phew!

As usual, huge thanks to the sparkling and talented Penguin publishing heroes, Reneé Naudé, Ziel Bergh, Ellen van Schalkwyk and Pam Thornley – rock stars! Thanks for all the patience, the late nights, the ever-changing schedules and the trust placed in me yet again. Told you not to worry, Reneé, one week behind schedule, and the best book by far!

A really big thank you has to go to the creative team at twoshoes (Quinton Bruton, Toby Attwell, Caterina Toffoli and Meghan Adams) for spending week upon week stuck in front of your screens. Thanks for working through the night and racing against time to get this book done. Not only did you make your deadline (again!), but you delivered yet another brilliantly thought-out and beautifully designed book. Beers are on me next time.

To Janet Gird, my fearless recipe tester – thank you for letting us make a mess in your kitchen and for the hours of research, testing and tweaking. (And for using your family as guinea pigs.) You're a real *staatmaker!*

To my brilliant photographer Louis Hiemstra – I know it's been a hard road – 50 000-odd photographs, late nights and having to fit in between the mayhem of filming the show . . . thanks for your amazing photographs.

Then a huge thank you to Oopsie and Dropsy: Helena Lombard and Caroline Gardner, my co-writer and food stylist respectively. I now think of the two of you as peas in a pod, complementing and driving each other forward. I don't know if I could've handled an 8000-kilometre road trip in your car (or a second helping of your mac and cheese), but this I do know: without you two crazy ladies, my life wouldn't be as rich or as interesting. Well done.

Lastly, special thanks to our sponsors, Pick n Pay (Bronwen Rohland, Malcolm Mycroft, Yvonne Short), Renault SA (Zavier Gobille, Fabien Payzan, Danielle Melville), Coca-Cola (Jodie Bailey-Norris, Marina Caldow, Ramokone Ledwaba) and Cadac (Elena Forno). Without your vision, there would be no book, no show and no thanks.

If I left anyone out – sorry! You can k*k me out at the next braai!

Justin

Index